I Survived
Auschwitz and Buchenwald

Memoirs of a Belgian Survivor
Of Nazi Concentration Camps

Louis Fynaut
Compilation: Paula Fynaut
Foreword: Paula Fynaut
Editors: Paula Fynaut, Paulino Lozada
Picture Cover: Historical View of Auschwitz
Dmitrijs Mihejevs/Shutterstock
© Paula Fynaut, 2014
ISBN: 978-0-9938893-1-8

Contents

The page contents indicate an approximation to the chronological events; the narrative sometimes go back and forth in time, depending on relevance, much the way events are stored in human memory.

Preface by Paula Fynaut:

After years of procrastination and postponements I finally bring to life my father's memoirs: Louis Fynaut, a Belgian youth who had moved to Nazi occupied France at the beginning of WW-II.

Subsequently, he was suspected by the Gestapo of taking part in the French resistance and considered dangerous. So he was designated N.N., Nacht und Nebel, night and fog, a political prisoners to be secretly transported to a forced labor concentration camp and, once he was no longer considered useful, banished without a trace.

First, he was carried to the infamous Auschwitz death camp, in occupied Poland, where he miraculously survived transportation, mistreatment, overwork, undernourishment and illness. Obviously he was considered valuable for slave labor and several months later he was transferred to Buchenwald, another camp within Germany. Ironically, his closest brush with death happened here, during an allied bombing raid.

After the end of the war Louis returned to Belgium where he was put on a nourishment program to build up his strength and allow him to be reintegrating into society. Unfortunately, many of his friends died during this recuperation period. Louis' stomach lining was ruined from starvation. Several doctors and medical professional were consulted but it was concluded that his stomach lining was beyond repair, and in his words, "I just learned to live with my weak stomach acids and get on with my life as best I could".

He wrote that, "At one point, during my rehabilitation in Belgium a dangerous boil materialized on the back of his neck, from where I have been stabbed during that terrible night in the barracks at Buchenwald when an image tried to frame me for something I had not done"! Fortunately this healed but for up to 5 years after his release he wrote that he experienced pain in his leg from an injury in the quarries in Buchenwald! My dad also wrote that it took a long time to receive any monetary compensation as the authorities were swamped with bogus claimants which blocked the process and consequently the legitimate suffers receiving their money in an expedient manner after the war!

After his rehabilitation he joined the Belgian Merchant Navy and eventually went to London, England and married. He had five children, four girls and one boy. From 1970 to 1989 he lived in South Africa and then Zimbabwe during the war years and up to and after Independence in 1981. He loved Africa and had a great passion for Africa and Geology which he pursued with fervor and great passion. Eventually, with his wife, he joined one of his daughters in Canada and had a happy and productive life until his death.

It is said that the big Oak stump situated at Buchenwald camp are the remains of Goethe's Tree; named thus because it is supposedly the tree under which he wrote "Wanderer's Nightsong" (Wandrers Nachtlied). I found this out while researching Buchenwald as I was thinking of visiting the site of my father's incarceration. After reading about Goethe, Buchenwald and the Oak Tree, I felt compelled to share my dad's memoir with other interested people. I believe he gained valuable insights though the experiences he endured during WW-II, which may be helpful to other people and institutions in the years to come.

Initially I contemplated the edition of his memoirs; they are written the way he expressed himself in English, with embodiments of his Flemish language. And they were typed so by my mother, in an age way before computers and automatic correction of grammar. I resisted this temptation and decided to stage them to the world in the manner they were initially conceived.

When I was a young girl in England in the 60's I was fascinated by the number tattooed on my Dad's arm. In recent years, after finally receiving his records from an institution namely, The Holocaust Museum in Washington D.C, it was confirmed that the number etched on his arm was indeed an Auschwitz number - 185590. To me, the memories of my dad and his Auschwitz number, symbolize his great courage and integrity, as well as the courage that others have faced while facing transforming circumstances. It is because my dad "Never Gave Up", that I am sitting here today and sharing his story. Voila!

Foreword:

My birth, soon after the first world war, 1923, at the beginning the depression was more a necessity than an accident as many of them were then produced, in a like manner. It took place in an attic with the sun's rays forcing themselves through the tiny roof window within the vicinity of the dockland yards.

It was ideally placed for any creature of future adventures to have a window on the world for which I would be gratefully hereafter installed, especially as the time would speed away and make the freedoms we would so much like to roll away like a vagrant hoop, leisurely proceeding at its own pace, pushed by its own impetus.

Growing up in the depression was like a last throwback to more primitive times. Education only at half strength was fully pursued with ardor, nevertheless with a phantom-like future, full of elusive illusions; the crystal ball was very cloudy in those times. No way out for betterment was seen or even emphasized. Coming events then would speak for themselves, to show us the way out of this chaotic and lethargic situation.

Luckily my youth was completely taken in by the coming change of wind, I don't know the reason.

By conclusive evidence of my own experience is that just being and the fact that my ancestors have demonstrated a high survival rate, like the sailors on the waves of the seas or similar to earthly explorer's wanderings, including those who have penetrated the zones of the air; it comes to the point that you have just got to be a survivor. One's poor presence is just enough sometimes to fill the contribution to the general influence of events on this planet.

One way or another life events happen to all of us and my personal participation in things well done gives me absolute satisfaction and contentment at having taken part in such events towards further constructive development. The eternal strife of good and evil encountered continued to be part of it all.

My baptismal ceremony was performed without my will and with no say in it, by my grandmother who made my father, the eldest son, to live up to his commitments and get married. I then became officially legalized and identified.

In this ritual of Christening the eldest son, according to my grandfather's tradition, was required to name his first born son "Emmanuel" the reason for this has still to be discovered. The day will dawn when we will; Anyway her fiery Flemish character took the upper hand and I became Louis, Emmanuel Fynaut.

The Fynaut's from Finaughty the Ulster-Dutch-Belgium connection was a far cry, from the French-Huguenots as some "think. She broke her umbrella over my grand- fathers head and I would have like to see it happen! Better not, I suppose, saving embarrassment but luckily I do not remember anything, just sound sleep and minding my own business through it all. My early growing pains were spent very comfortably the center of everybody's attention and feeling like a kind of *wunderkind* or prince but far removed from any princedom soaking it all up and enjoying temporarily a fill up to my ego.

I could not go wrong until my adolescent pangs showed up as individualism and fierce independence for endeavoring on my own into the wide world. Suddenly, all worldly attention was lost, opposition unleashed, experiencing instead the combined attack of the whole family from every side.

No more pie in the sky for me, on the contrary, I had to start fighting for a more painful survival against   hostility of this worldly existence coming at me from the pits of darkness.

One of my closest friends *Achilles* pointed out one day to me "God is all around us", and from then on I never lost that consciousness, like it was there all the time. My accidents would increase at an alarming rate with the risks, but my survival rate was good.

Roofs and drainpipes would collapse and drop off with me attached. I was reckless, carefully learning to calculate because many were the painful experiences. The falls and knocks on the head took the shape of a flat design on the back that started to bother me s or could it be hereditary factors at work.

My family tree wasn't all bad, as a matter of fact I became impressed. From lawyers to Police Commissioners and farmers on my grandmother's side to army Vets, captains and seafarers and farmers on my father's side. From my mother's side, seigneurs, merchants and farmers: that's the French connection.

One of my grandfather's relations got intermarried into a baronage going back to Charlemagne's time namely Van Monchoven's for Flandre du Nord and Peqque in Hainaut.

My own tendencies are inclined to be humane and like Francis of Assisi, nice with an affinity for animals or like some American Indians, some of which existed in my mother's side of the family, very sensitive.

Animals come and talk to me like they are almost chattering back to me by mutual feelings more than consent, the fish to silently accepting and appreciating the nature ways, they could feel the awareness, those feelings my mother felt very strongly. This was not all a figment of the imagination, in real human terms it was definitely a lovely sensation taught to them one by one. Proof to find was most difficult to do or comprehend on this subject as it all came by impulse. The negative was most influenced by a lot of envy.

I have come to the conclusion that this is still because of our position in the universe. Improvement will come as we progress content with our passing through towards better enlightenment and comprehension further ahead as we meet the many   confrontations.

Introduction:

It is easier to justify one's birthright than the way our academic education was played about with only terrible thing to contemplate. Although, we had more possibilities than our parents ever had but the current social standards at that time caused us to lose our drive to get ahead and to persevere. Being put in the bridle of a hard day's work together with a good bit of discipline as is the trouble again today.

Our ambitions were let down. We heard over and over again the grisly war tales of our fathers, artillery, machine gun fire, bayoneting, gas, Spanish Flu, cholera, cruelty, starvation and all the combined suffering. We felt we wouldn't endure or stand up like them.

At the height of those big crisis or depressions it gave us nothing to look forward to, except cheap living but without aim or ambitions. The films, with their glamour and illusion as in the roaring twenties, were full of action where people were dancing and fairs were around, gave us part of our education I would say. Otherwise, as youngsters we had no money for anything, we were paupers, we had to earn everything the hard way. Just as well as that gave us something to fight for.

Drugs were unheard of, kept well away in the far-East and only used by the upper crust. There was discipline on hard drinking and pubs were well controlled and whatever we earned and by whatever means there was, there was never enough over for romantic liaisons; again you had to dare and win and take your chances. The girls were only interested in security and inheritances. So like the rovers of old we had to go a-Viking. The syllabus of the High School helped to drain the extra energy but all in all it had no prospects except for those geniuses that would lose their hair on it, or those that had something to acquire like their father's business.

I chose the difficult way as there was nothing my parents could help with. As they couldn't place me in the marine school, which practically assured one a job in the fishing fleet or in the coastguard, for which my Mother tried hard enough. We soon found out that the sons of the inland sugar-daddies took the glamour bit they thought it to have. Actually the war was a time for action and a hidden calamity which disguised the opportunity it would bring to draw forth the men of action.

1- Early years in Belgium:

During the long pause of slackness we had learned to man the boats bringing the fishermen in from their trawlers, acquire the best fish and eels out of creeks, rivers and bays. Even sell some of the extra stock and breed mussels in large quantities, near the sluices, which were as big as the palm of your hands, catch wild fowl, mostly ducks and starlings and hares in the dunes and it's open spaces, Roaming around then, picking berries in season. The rest of the game had vanished in previous times due to overpopulation, except in the Ardennes. Instead we started to gather old iron from industrial scrapheaps and sold that to make a penny more.

My first bicycle came from all of this collecting, so I was able to go to High school again, the institution where you paid for your books and had to be decently dressed instead of being out of tune with your peers. My father didn't have to pay High school fees as he was unemployed at the time.

We managed to make our own athletic equipment, scrounged oars and planks put together, iron rings from triangle time ringers, lead in sackcloth for halters and we had just two pairs of boxing gloves from my uncle Gerard who had emigrated to Canada, to cover that need. We ran the mile around the railroad fences, we called that the bilges which were railroad sleepers and the planks we took from the woodpiles in the dockyards of the Norwegian-Swedish ships.

There was also a lumpy field to play soccer on and javelins were made from the trees in a small park which had gone wild. Throwing discs formed from iron slack in the furnaces. We were victorious in all our competitions and if not we fought it out afterwards. Sometimes it had to be stopped by teachers or even the police, very exciting that was. Although we had no recognition as such although we formed the cadres of the best teams in comparison with the others.

The organized teams of the snobs mostly in town had no equals at all in competition compared with to our stronger athletes who would form the bulk of the resistance later.

The snobs or sugar-daddy's sons misrepresented our hidden strengths as well inside the country and abroad – what a shocking state of affairs that was. It was even a pity looking at it, most of them couldn't even make one hand stand or haul themselves up to the parallel bars most of them.

Our soccer teams were better than any of theirs and so I could go on and on, the letdown was disastrous. Most of all our fighting was up to the quick S.A.S. Standards and not just street fighting.

Even the Army didn't have our foresight. Again because of the same wrong leadership created through nepotism and corruption. Their schools didn't encourage open and free practices of development, Rather to be seen sneaking and tittle tattling to the teachers was encouraged which stopped the strive towards more open thinking and advancement. It was the stuff from which Charles De Koster's book was written which was against the Spanish occupation. We had not got rid of the lethargy caused by the inquisition. The prerogative of the neighboring nations, inhibited by the bias of Spaniards, Austrians, French and Germans the same over history has proved what we cannot always count on our allies to help as out either, which, in our history has been more often than not. One dictatorship is not different from the other and if we are not already prepared to fend it off with our own initiative and continuous regeneration of resources then we are not worth it.

All those youth organizations, I remember starting from the Boy-Scouts, Kajotters or the Red-Falcons. I couldn't even afford a whistle, notwithstanding the protocol and pomp for the adults, the secret societies and guilds all old fashioned and antique now.

2- Pre-War Political Climate:

Only the Syndicates, federations and unions survived and in some ways the Mafiosi were doing better. Badly equipped in this position we waited for the onslaught of a new order out of old foundations; regeneration not as benefactors of mankind but of total corruption suppressing the masses to a former state.

While the Red-Falcons were singing "never no more war for those big lords, let them try". The Kajotters wearing their Papal ensign, singing to the past former Roman glory with appeasement to this order; the liberals with their scouts still living in the Boer-war, which also was a travesty. Over the border Eastward in contrast the very dark clouds were gathering unhindered by an ill wind of catastrophic forebodings. Had we not heard of the screams and cries of its crushed victims and closed our ears accordingly.

This wind brought thunder and lightning to the now unprepared after the other. "The Blitz"! It was called. The fully prepared new gangsters and bullies with a new invigorated army of willing soldiers known for their war-like tendencies marching to victory and oblivion at the same time, jack booting over everybody and singing away.

Black because it liked that color, a broken light drifting away from its eternal source by multiple distortions. The lessor obstructions would destroy it; because of their ability to receive again and giving further light. The collision and destruction would shatter the irregularities so the surviving would have continuity for further momentum and harmony. A balance had to be found for all striving and then the emanations can go forward and back unhindered.

Knowing the oneness of the infinitive in purpose. The last bastion and port of call for us would then be the only remaining fortress with such natural qualities endowed so as to fight the reactionary forces brought into existence from a long line of adverse circumstances.

This drive would really force us into action; expressed by patriotism and a high esteem for freedom and justice. As the struggle intensified, all kind of fraction units would be brought to life coming to a coalition. First of all the Belgian soldiers, prisoners of Flemish extraction returning, by an ethnical statement made by Hitler himself, that all Flemish had to be considered as real Germans. Something that gave us a lot of trouble by the ignorant and easy led chauvinists from the opposite. The White Brigades and other resistance groups would be formed. The Communists only came in one year later, under orders of Stalin. Individual patriots would look up contacts and act on their own, trusting nobody. All would work for the same cause. The ultimate for many would be to reach the fighting forces overseas. The chosen would come back as agents, of which there was soon a small efficient army now born.

The calling and sacrifice was remarkable. Many of the youngsters were of the same cadres that would have gone in the army anyway, 1943. The status would be political and documented as spying by the enemy for taking arms up against them, which goes for both sides. Afterwards we would be considerably our own as having completed army service during the war years and equalized with the regular forces.

Never accepting defeat was our own decision in action, we knew the consequences and the cost, paying with our lives, if caught. The importance of this contribution cannot be emphasized enough seeing that we were already there and constituted a threefold hidden force. Refractions the French called it.

Some would stay and fight in the resistance or the marquis. When a meeting was accomplished others would become passeurs, saboteurs and keepers of safe-houses, couriers, etc. The network was extent and singularly in cells organized but held together by its tentacles.
Eventually joining the official forces was the better way of fighting back. The other was just as important to the war effort. Both attributed to each other.

If caught execution on the spot was the immediate ordeal in the beginning, but the need of interrogations by torture was increasingly practiced when the S. D. The "*Seckerheits Dienst*", branch of Gestapo started to take control, from there you were lucky, one may say if you reached the concentration camp alive. Also as the secret army started increasing and replacing the executed and disappearing victims, with war going in reverse and afraid of reprisals now the Germans used them as long as they, could for slave labor and replacement of their own diminishing multitudes in the work force, proved to be a cheap handy replacement.

3- The Blitz:

The "Blitz", was a well prepared affair. To take everybody off guard, as weak as they were in internal strife, divided and softened up. The pre conditioning of Germany was well done, rare in its crude form like a Tartar Steak, supplied by all the right ingredients worked out to a fine art of surprise attack.

What surprised me and most people I imagine was the fact, what despite all the warning signs we were still so vulnerable. Engrossed in our own world, nicely tucked away leaving the unguarded entry's open and barricading the old ones with a straw fence.

The drift of breaking out from the East and center was always westward first. History had proven that. Civilization moved, westwards and comes back to the east after encompassing the earth. Nationalism, racism, chauvinism, politics wars and revolutions all based on greed. All the psychology, pomp and glamour including the cruelty, murder and atrocities enhancing it to unrivalled proportions and magnitude.

On the other hand the crude adventure and vitality released was unheard of since Viking times, a share it was wasted but the chance taking compensated for the bloodletting. Some had the time of their lives. Shooting, plundering, exterminating, and declaring it was all everybody else's fault in an orderly and disciplinary way.

Achieving the same motive, repeated as before it looked a continuation with a pause and entente between the big wars. The same overcoats and fellows in them or their sons. Standards improved) gunnery the one that they won the West with, excellent air cover and a tank shield for their infantry trimmed to a precision with disruptive forces sowing discord: the fifth columnists and then a submarine fleet to cut off the supplies.

The rush to the beaches was on since the start, never mind the cost. His revenge above all else. If he had a short time to enjoy it, like Nero, at least make the most of it.
This syndrome drove the great machine along taking as much as they could in their wake. The whole mass of overproduction seen since the industrial revolution to a near quagmire proportion. A self-destructing Frankenstein, juggernaut. No good could come out of this except by another reaction stronger than this one created, which evolved out of

the abyss by counter revolutions and coalitions of an allied unity as human kind had never seen before. The awakening took place in a furor of counter measures unheard off once attained. For every destructive undertaking there was another one more efficient and bigger than the first one.

The unemployment crumbled on all sides rapidly and organized might achieved miracles within a stone throw, the opposing forces unleashed and killed the myth, that nationalization cannot solve the countries ills, it very well did on both sides.

In seven years Hitler built a force that challenged the world, and the world one that destroyed him in a shorter time. Then war or peace, what are the odds for creating the same. Everybody did his homework and the possibilities were found for everything. It was overdone, but achieved the aims.

The individual houses fell one after the other, across the water the islands held steadfast and became the bulwark for everybody. Its reserves were gigantic and not depleted. The monster had to look into its backyard to find an equalizer which meant more bloodletting for its army running on borrowed time and manpower at the exhaustive stage now. The rest of the globe was still picking up the momentum like a big wheel brought in motion.

Beware of everything in between those colossuses from stalemate and quantum to all sides around to squash the death center, nothing could hold this gigantic creation of a combined intelligence, material and armies ready to crush the common enemy and this danger forever more.

Never mind the screaming, singing and marching. The ball was rolling and turned the other way. I remember from the calm before the storm, the fifth column had free reign, in our poor democracy of apathy widespread in our own backyard of nationalistic groups and sponsors. The fence sitters and do-goodies all enjoying the last supper of calamities.

I was in the position to observe from my window, like an astonished owl with bewildered wisdom, watching how the acrobatic masters trained crews of the late Strassburger circuses, did the rounds of countries, just before all hell broke loose, taking photos of all our weak military places with installations openly exposed.

There was also a big modern U.S.A. windjammer called .the "Sea Cloud" regularly doing the beat between Ostend and Monaco, closely followed by the "Vanadis", a fair sized modern motor yacht, owned by a Greek shipping magnate. We knew the crew of both very well, as good customers. Mostly German speaking on the former and on the other was Captain Sven Rasmussen a well-known international spy secretly monitoring the Sea-Cloud surrounded by a shroud. The U.S.A. Ambassador to Brussels took swiftly off on it, just before the invasion, without much ado and noise as the last clarion call was sounded. Known, in some old fashioned well-guarded established quarters, there was a certain amount of intrigue going on, I would say of great expectations but of a "laissez-faire" attitude. After all Hitler with his bullies may be still a kind of liberator putting the clock back toward old privileges of the ruling right. What you know, to be born to live such destiny as the apprentice to the wizard, putting their houses in order again, but going wild and uncontrolled power drunk; driving his donkey and offspring to the sea and to "drang nach Osten" with lots of "Lebensraum" to spare, cutting down the new red giant and running on from there: expending his own fury while the West could rearm and concentrate all of its might in a concerted effort towards the final push leaning on its enormous reserves. That's how it worked out with the angels and devils working overtime at it.

Our intelligences were very much alike with their hands tied behind their backs waiting. Anyway everybody had a good time and might as well enjoy it before the explosion erupted.

Life was very economical, food was cheap, no Work but the unemployment pay kept everybody going and my grandmother's Cafe did a roaring trade with people dancing away their worries day and night. The last of the old ways mingled with the embryo of the new age. Rents were cheap but not many amenities were provided.

Everybody wanted to live it up, tourists all over the place. It could have gone on forever but it was too good to be true. The Fuhrer and his generals were preparing their set, unhindered by all this levity.
A little incident maybe, of bigger proportions and consequences to be later than we thought at the time happened in an eerie and phantom like manner, accidently but almost looking prearranged.

King Albert managed to fall from loose rocks on Marche-Les-Dames in spite of the fact that he was an experienced climber, good strategist and of strong character. King Albert could very well figure out the German way of thinking, past mastery of military strategy and tactics were at his fingertips.

King Leopold, his son, was brought up in a monastery like atmosphere of doubtful influences which undermined all positive thinking which was so much needed on our side.

Queen Astrid's death was more like an unhappy reckless unwanted accident which again carried suspicious undertones: gossip going the full round among the populace. People speculating that the car could have been tampered with like the mountain rocks was of no help. The shadows were there, flickering, the sinister prelude of the reign of terror, its tentacles spreading like an octopus of gigantic proportions.

The people's premonitions of bad things are more often than not the revelations of what we cannot see and understand in the offing. So the time-bomb went on ticking away. Our defensive measures under King Albert's auspices would have been much better than what we had after his long fall to the bottom anyway.

I envisage with the necessary finances available he would have made of Belgium one strong fort protecting both military and civilians to withstand any superior beleaguering from the suspect eastern frontier especially and then all around fortify against further encirclement.

His Albert Canal was an excellent idea if backed up and also Eben-Email the cornerstone to the rocky Walloon Ardennes. An entire population could have hidden in those Ardennes and the dunes stretching along the coast, cities could have been re-walled using the old ones, protective measures as in olden times intertwining with each other. In a prolonged siege we would have lost our armament industry for sure as it is situated on the very same border Eastwards, but we could have expected help and sustainment from our allies and stay as a buffer stone and springboard as before. Maybe just as well not to as the total destruction would have been catastrophic on the face of the land and the combined mafia styled intrigue must have seen to it that it would not happen. The good and the right go first, it never fails. "To Each His Own".

The French with their part of the Maginot-Line, making it a proper laughing stock which the German Thrust Stratagem proved at Eben-Email: they would make a show piece of it.

Since King Albert's death nothing further had been done to it obviously, which made some corners and crannies vulnerable to any well prepared enemy concentration, exactly to the point that it was what the German Command did, in charge of the operations with a mock up, exposing all the weaknesses well trained and rehearsed before the attack, after a softening up by the *Luftwaffe*, with the help of a *"Big Bertha"* brought near the site.

By then the Belgians were locked in, unable to shoot from their slits in the walls, that were the weak points, the Achilles' heel. The demolition squads could come right in under the wall placing their explosives, moving from crater to crater under cover while in the meantime the para-troops were getting ready to land on top of the fort as it had no air cover.

All this lasted three days with the General Walking out, and most of his troops, carrying his sword and pistol in honor of his most disastrous defense. The Germans admiring the tenacity against the enormous odds, fully aware of the impact in close combat, which they had witnessed. After this the Belgian regulars had thirty German divisions to reckon with, immensely superior in weaponry. The Sappers neutralizing the bridges over the Albert Canal as the pillar boxes were being destroyed by stukas, deniers and combined pinpointed artillery fire in a non-stop raid, relentlessly bombing roads and the population which was moving along it; unchallenged.

The promised allied backing was nowhere in view and as soon as the first German attack started in earnest a complete right turn was commanded and whipped along with the knowledge of Rommels break through at Sedan in the French Ardennes, and the flight was on.

On hearing that news, the French divisions made an even quicker turn as they had not made any significant advance on Belgian territory unlike the B.E.F. The French never filled in the gap between the Maginot Line and the Belgian Ardennes.

Eben-Email with further along the Albert Canal towards Zeeland over Antwerp, making an ideal first defensive line left was the only thing. The Meuse would have done the rest with the sheer cliffs on the Western side of the river. Rommel drove just along it on the other side, his tank column more or less waving to the Belgian troops in their fortified citadels as they passed by, till they reached the gap near the Luxemburg border taking the protective corridors in the gap near the Luxemburg border taking the protective corridors inwards finding the last valleys with no resistance wide open for them. Appearing at Sedan in France on hard opened undulating terrain, ideal for their new heavier tanks and articulated artillery. From there it was a glorified hike over the Hunruck, this part was only filled with horse regiments and smaller tanks with a limited operation range man and commanded by an upcoming subaltern, a determined fighter, the late Charles De Gaulle.

In the meantime, the Dutch had completely collapsed in the North, outmaneuvered by the parachuters over the flooded area near the border, the destruction of Rotterdam and their own unpreparedness leading to a swift downfall.

Belgium was encircled with Allies on the run holding a flimsy rear guard action with the Belgians in the forefront relentlessly retreating to were both reactions could join up, the Germans had to deal with fierce fighting from that quarter before advancing again, enabling the B.E.F. to make it to Durnkirk, passing the refugee columns suffering on the regular strafing and bombardment.

The Schliessen plan was completely circumnavigated spurring the Flemish troops who were being pushed back in this futile attempt to make something of it against thirty divisions.

The French of course liked to blame us for experiencing, some British politicians eagerly sitting on the bandwagon, buttering up to a bigger ally knowing very well that the agreement condoned this retreat in the event of total overwhelming.

The Germans had done their own meticulously and therefore provisions were let down in anticipation of this happening and indeed it did; intelligence was aware of this considering that there was more than the eye could see.

The Agreement concluded that in irreversible circumstances Lord Gort would liaison between the British High Command, Lord General Allenbrook and the Belgian king's army headquarters; the order would be a tactical retreat as good as the situation permitted, which the king followed till the last soldier had got off those beaches and he was to capitulate as planned.

There was no condition attached as to what he should do afterwards, unless a stand was made, he chose to stay with his people. Unlike General's Montgomery's suggestion that he was going to take the Belgian Officers in custody and take command over them.

Lord Allanbrooke knew exactly the independent spirit of the Belgians deciding against it. Lord Allenbrooke's memoirs elaborate widely on this subject and the very revealing events in this phase of the war.

The other suggestion was that the remaining Belgian contingents could rejoin the French throughout Rommels line was hopelessly out of order too, we never could have run that fast in all sincerity. Our eighteen days campaign was longer than anybody, considering the Dutch gave in and fell in four days: the British fled to fight another day and the French eighteen times bigger with five times more population and far more divisions in the field than we could ever mobilize in so short a time span, gave up in twenty four days: just six days longer than us. On top of that the B. E. F. was let go by Hitler, everybody knows about his peculiar ways. The credit goes really to the rear-guards who fought heroically and in most instances to the last ditch being indiscriminately annihilated.

The stupid ignorance and accusations in silly mudslinging circle and released by the press was a pitiful display by the politicians, as well, followed by the disappointment of the multitude still dipped in the throes of frustration which would be a handicap for some time to come.

To this day we still do not understand very well the full implications of this behavior which is still practiced.

On the surface of it all it looked like an enormous fiasco, accomplished, in the enemy's favor.

The stand at the Yzer Front by the Belgians in the First World War was in no way comparable to the sudden departure of the B. E. F. at Dunkirk. The Luftwaffe's use of air power achieved a lot which was unchallengeable. They had a ball and used it to the hilt. The refugee columns were a hinderance to us congesting the roads and the Germans taking advantage of it. On the other hand the retreating army useless and mingled with the crowds. Another suggestion was to fight behind the cities, towns and villages as proposed by our allies. The Belgians didn't like that idea any more than in the time of the Duke of Marlborough and preferred to fight in front, middle and lastly at the rear. There is a great difference when you are on your home ground. The terror the bombers were ordered to practice on civilians was another important factor, a preconceived conclusion in war of this kind for speedy results. No adequate protection was provided or organized for this tactic, the existing ditches and strong buildings were a great help. The remaining buildings from the middle ages were still the best to hide in with their vaults.

Since the beginning of the "Blitz" the weather had been splendid, sunshine galore, blue skies warmth and one of the best summers in memory. The only black clouds were the grey flying machines with black crosses and pilots who manned them with grinning faces like the Apocalypse horses, with an ugly appearance of doom and despair in the sky. Big columns of grey coated regulars passing under it moving automatically like robots to nowhere, ready to create death and do massacres. It was like something extinguished "Our Freedom". Everybody wanted to be at Dunkirk. It was like a swarm of Bees around a honeypot.

Our little country contemplating the engulfment by subversion of another temporary and short Dark-Age: cut off and coming to a standstill. The cross-roads and heart was having one of its sporadic setbacks and had to sleep now.

The shimmering lights which heated the air currents over the North Sea were going down to a glimmer.

How often had I looked at this wonder of nature on my comfortable branch in my favorite tree on the summit of the little park pondering on the recurring subject of "Quo Vadis". On looking down under the tree I saw a thief hiding his loot and before I could get down and do something about it he quickly ran away, he was later caught without my help but I wish I could have done something about it. It could have been hazardous but one must try at all times and not be too slow or in doubt when it comes to action.

Wrongdoing needs to be brought into the open and declared, nevertheless, there are certain reservations one must contemplate, "the church has to stay in the center of the village" was the old saying. In my case don't fall from the tree doing it. My tree was a safe place while it lasted. I think it is still there and not gone into oblivion. Big bombs exploded around it, strafing the little wood, to no avail, it was indestructible.

I have done what I dreamed off in the safety of its green foliage: I followed the long coast-line from Europe to the extremities of South Africa, by sea, air and overland and came back after it all to the same place.

The America's are not a strange continent for me, like my ancestors travelling, I have done the journey to familiar lands, far and wide towards the horizon. In no time Ostend became a transit harbor and also open city, this statement is made on its military importance, I never could reconcile that with the reality.

A heavy French anti-air machine gun was placed not far from tree, from this the missiles rained down and the soldier manning it was never found afterwards. I found it prudent to get down as quickly as possible as the soldier maneuvering with the gun sight could have got me out of that tree even quicker.

Refugees endlessly streaming by now from the Eastern borders telling us about the murderous strafing they had encountered everywhere.

The Messerschmitt's pilots liked to zig-zag low over the countryside playing games, shooting at anything they saw moving. They came swooping over the dunes in a surprise attack. One day with our French soldier having his hands ready full with all sides shooting at once and his gun getting overheated was finally killed by a big bomb that a Dornier had dropped right in front of him. Around us the big bullets were flying and ricocheting making a hellish noise, rattling everything about us.

I was just helping a neighbor's wife with her pram and baby in it to get them quickly downstairs and we just reached the little cellar in time. That was our first baptism of fire I reckon, the next one was soon to follow in the evening as we were contemplating in the twilight a few high flying planes taking our deep attention.

We always could tell after a time by the heavier droning which planes were ours or which were the enemies: all of a sudden in their wake we noticed two gigantic explosions in the barquentine where the mail boats regularly embarked from. It really lit up the whole area, vividly nice garlands of fireworks sprouting from it in every direction, these were mines not bombs that had floated silently from them.

The quickness of the events suddenly gave me the wish to be in Canada with my youngest uncle Gerrard and aunt Esther who had both left our shores at an early stage and established themselves there. How nice for them they would miss the fire-works maybe someday I would tell them about it.

The same stories like my Father and Uncle Louis, both veterans of the last war, having won their laurels and Yzer-Cross decorations. What the hell, all over again, it was in retrospect like a slow motion of the same power continuing the last war.

Our studies in High School had abruptly ended, welcomed by most students like a vacation and some had even sung patriotic songs on the announcement of the ultimatum, so moving it always is that it brought tears to our eyes. I also felt sorry for all people especially the mothers, when I jumped on my bicycle that memorable day and sped homeward.

I was disappointed by the sight of some of our weaponry passing by, moving towards the front.

It looked more like old museum pieces than anything else, actually it was. That, with our old biplanes dropping out of the sky just before, or flying in the target practice bags by lack of maneuverability was just enough to give us the worst hopes of what was in store to tackle the fast and agile Messerschmitt. Versatile all round articulated guns poised on us and on their way already, as we realized and pondered. My Mother was of the same thought and a foreboding of pending disaster quickly closing in had her plans at the ready when the witan or gathering of elders came together: the old people's council as we say. To begin with my Mother never liked the sea she was possessed of an absolute abhorrence of the wide waters and had delusions of drowning in it.

4- Some Family Background:

My Dad's family and Grandmother were more close to the sea since the dawn of history so for them it was the water and traditionally England that was the course to follow.

In the years 1914-1918 they had gone there too. My grandfather joined the convoys for supplies to the front and my Dad and Uncle's for the Anny. One Uncle was torpedoed on the way to South-West-Africa, this was my Uncle Edward, the youngest died from scarlet fever after winning the athletic championship in London for his Grammar School that was Alphonse and Gerrard worked in, Claridge's Hotel of London as a waiter.

They had sailed the North Sea in a fishing boat taking one of the cousins with them from my Grandmother's brother, Oscar, staying behind after the war and marrying an English girl.

Anyway somehow my mother convinced them all that it was better to take the way along to Dunkirk, if possible, to the Panne and then to London, the safer road by a long shot.

One of the reasons in this suggestion was also the broadcast on the Belgian Radio announced by this hour of emergency that all young men of army age should keep themselves ready and proceed to the nearest point of Dunkirk to be able to make a last ditch stand. So they would stay with me; my Mother meant.

My Mother previously also had worked with an Armenian ammunition magnate from Paris who had told her that she and her family could come there and work for him, so she had definitely had the right connections. There were always Armenians. She had been impressed as a child with the friendly southern comfort and that influence had stayed with her I remember. This was an open invitation to prove it. The die was cast and we packed with all haste.

When we were ready the picture we made was a bit theatrical, our best clothes and those bright woolen blankets around our shoulders, big cases with our belongings; I started to hate carrying baggage ever since even for holidays: saying goodbye to the old friendly house and giving the keys to the neighbors who were more known for actual piracy than anything else. I saw them just smiling behind that mask of delightful sincerity, but on the other hand knowing very well the fierce temper of my grandmother if and when she would come back to be cautious and that sooner or later they would have that to contend with, so that made for a reasonable balance in this barter, not to go over the mark.

As was expected, the rear action was no match for the German push, all that it managed to do was to slow them down a bit and to regroup every so often, careful not to fall into an unforeseen ambush.

Our Flemish looks made us very German-like in appearance which would be taken against us in this phony war and proving to be an unkind ethnic handicap. This would make us the more determined to be ourselves as we advanced towards Belgian soil and made it easier for us to return home.

We were not interested in immediate assimilation with others we didn't feel akin to or them to us. I think we went through the same trauma and experiences the Jewish people had gone through: the position of our country being somehow similar to the old Canaan and Israel.

Our branch of the Fynaut's in the Netherlands including Belgium had been intermarried all over, from the Van Monchhovens for Hainaut and Northern-France: owning small castles and textile factories in Pecque and Roubaix to subsidiaries in Casablanca, Morocco.

Then we had my first cousin Irene, daughter of my Uncle Louis and Aunt Rachele Pauwaert, renowned old Icelandic seafarers, the Grandfather was either lost on the high seas, thrown overboard or started another family in Reykjavic and was never seen again.

My cousin was married or rather sold as such to a Jewish merchant known in Casablanca who owned two shops for ship repairs one in Casablanca and the other in Rabat. The family suspected him of being a white slave trader and drug dealer with connections in Rio de Janeiro.

Humphrey Bogart must have been featured after him, My Aunt Ray also resembled Mae West the way she played the part and ruined my Uncle in prohibition times, in Canada over Lake Eerie to the U.S.A. His tobacco farm was broke, tractor driven in the ditch and sending a couple of Mafia thugs to kill him. We never knew what happened but by the looks of him on his return to his homeland with tattered clothes and working his way over from New York on an old steamer shoveling coal in the ovens for the big boiler, we guess that he just about made it, dodging the wrath of the teamsters union and their henchmen.

Very likely he made them pay dearly for it, too. We heard of my Uncle Gerrard one day that the police were still looking for his whereabouts after a very uncomfortable investigation he had at the border of New York State whilst visiting.

As soon as my Uncle Louis had saved a good bit on the pilot-ships, happy by himself, my Aunt Ray appeared on the scene again, helping herself to his money and her Mother's at the same time; how foolish he was. My cousin was shoveled in between both, during that process and they became caught in the occupation, for a while a blessing in disguise.

5- Life in Occupied Belgium:

Arriving early morning at the quay to take the coastal train we were amazed at the devastation caused by mines and explosions from the evening before. This train was like a long electric tram with lots of carriages taking us as far as De Panne "La Panne" as the French call it near the border.

The Ostend fleet had mostly left loaded to the brim with their own crews and families. Melancholy descended over us as we said Goodbye to most people we knew, only one boat hit a mine and all were rescued from this disaster.

The planes were busy following us, covered by those big yellow blankets, coming from miles beyond the eastern horizon. The trip to De Panne was uneventful passing well known places and landmarks. We were joined by more family members from both sides of the family. My father's originally came from Kaaskerke near Diksmuide and Boezinge near Ypres, so well known as "Flanders Fields".

My Father did his war service in 1914 at the very same spot where my Grandfather was born and also he spent his own holidays in a nice little homestead that also provided a ferry to cross the river Yzer, the exact location where the Belgian Army faced the German forward post, just fifty yards away and where they got stopped in the attack by the flooding, caused by opening the sluices at high tide in Newport at the right time sinking the heavy German artillery and men in the slimy mud with the only alternative left to them to climb in the trees, to be mercilessly shot out of them.

From there the front straightened itself up angle wise right to the Swiss border for four terrible years and the Schliesen-plan was completely thwarted and buried in the morass of Flanders.

How a small cornerstone could make all the difference, the possible one of the Kaiser's downfall in the West. This time however we only caught up with the first throngs of refugees hiding the widespread sand dunes over at "De Panne" meaning a flat depression. There was no transport available from here, just plain footslogging for the rest of the way. All extra weight had to be discarded in the first pan we had chosen for night cover, staying in a safe flat depth among the sand hills. The good weather was well with us and we decided to continue next morning ever forward. Before the evening fell I decided to venture a bit around while my Dad went to the shops to get bread and other supplies.

This was once part of the wild pirate-coast used by all invaders from their harsh lands towards better grounds and also famous smugglers like, Jan Baert. Wide long beaches without interruptions, strong prevailing western winds for sail carting on the beach, racing was instituted and was started by my Mother's uncle, Edmund Clarysse, small beginnings from a bicycle shop which rented out to tourists expanded into a garage on new premises and then manufactured the sail carts using bicycle wheels. All her brothers became champions dedicated to this sport. We could have done with a couple of them I thought tackling in the western breeze towards our destination. Suddenly my daydreaming was interrupted, drawn upward by fighter planes battling each other in my full view.

The dog-fight was between one coastal British patrol and an overbearing pompous Messerschmitt, cocksure of itself meeting the British plane. Mind you it didn't take long before the Spitfire or whatever it was got the better of him and to our utter enjoyment shot him down. A billowing white object released itself from which dangled a small black dot as the stricken plane plummeted to earth some distance away, drifting towards the inward open   countryside. His landing couldn't have possibly been contemplated to be anywhere near our spot as the wind took him further inland. Nevertheless as I looked at some old German maps I had found in before my Grandmother's cupboard/departure was considered.

I now decided to check our position on these excellent maps. All of a sudden appearing from nowhere a rubicund little lady French speaking came near me, all excited gesticulating towards another group like herself: in no time surrounding my innocent person and pointing now to me holding this old German map.

Actually the Germans had repaid us with them after having so irresponsibly destroyed our old towns, cities and lands so fiercely defended by the Belgian soldiers, mostly Flemish judging by the names on gravestones of the, fallen. Anyhow those panicky citizens, accusing me in my own region, and in my own country without much ado are the biggest let down of the lot spewing the seeds of discord. To take me for a German parachutist, who was blown a couple of miles away was an act of complete stupidity and no decent excuse can be found for citizens who do not recognize their own inhabitants in a bilingual country.

Luckily my Mother and Grandmother arrived simultaneously on the scene after hearing all the poise and could prove my identity and innocence and my Dad arrived to verify that it had to be seen. My Grandmother a real fighter soon put this group to shame for their ignorance and they scattered like cackling hens.

They were lucky that we had no time for them. We had a good laugh about sitting around the campfire during supper, never mind the planes and war now. We settled down for a healthy night's sleep. The first one to remember under the starry sky. This was the 10th of May, 1940 my birthday.

"L;Etienne Cordiale" left still much to be desired in a little country like ours. Religion would blow that up to unreasonable proportions if and when it suited likewise politics. It was in the spirit of a "Lamme Goedzack" as Tyl Uilenspiegel' s best friend that we could withstand the inquisitions and occupations.

The might of resistance could not be borne by this flimsy incident of a mob bent on sensationalism. Men of action would again hopefully pull towards higher ideals.

With parachutists everywhere we were a potential enemy in their eyes and they became afraid of their own shadows. The media was a lot to blame for that. After this small incident, the next day saw us "en route", more seriously for Dunkirk again commonsense thrown to the winds and whatever premonitions we might have harbored ignored.

We proceeded on the road which divided the Dunes and Folder ground following in the footsteps of a miserable multitude, head and backs bent, noses burning in the sun, trudging along we could have sung the boat song but instead the sighing was stronger than the Volga flowing gently to the Black Sea.

Suddenly a low flying plane of unrecognizable markings appeared over our heads and although it made a small stir in the masses nobody moved towards the ditches, possibly most had seen the tri-color, I had not from where I was. I was the only one jumping for the ditch to the laughing concern of the nearest crowd who turned out to be our accusers of the day before. The French planes became one of the rarest sights we had had for some time.

My father called me back and made me feel ashamed of myself I could have crawled back into my skin. Our nerves were all on edge by that time. Solemnly and relentlessly the human ribbon kept on the move, passing a huge chemical factory which the Germans preserved in anticipation of further use to them.

All over the land we had those contrasts since the beginning of the hostilities, Humans indeed were far more dispensable than that. By nightfall we reached one of the very ancient large farms left with a group of black robed priests and nuns nervously praying and walking agitatedly about. A whole cloister on the move to Brittany in France for the duration of the war.

We all found shelter on top of the big granary they usually had for storage of hay, banquets, weddings and funerals. The big strong farmer shaking his head saying he would never move whatever came. His crops were coming on nicely and that was the only thing worthwhile that mattered to him.

In the meantime Dornier bombers and British fighters had decided to fight it out just near the sea and over the dunes a spectacle to behold. Some of the Dorniers displaying their black markings soon went down in red flaming pieces with various parts swiveling around, the Nuns and Priest increasing the velocity of their prayers with increasing ardour praying for the lost souls and us too, I hope.

Later on as dusk was falling we saw the silhouette of trains coming from inland moving towards Westhook of Oost-Dunkerke. The farmer informed us that this had been going on for several evenings with the wounded and dying soldiers, mostly Belgians from the quickly falling fighting zones. That's how the battle was raging for those in it; fierce and unyielding.

This was the prelude of the air battle over Dunkirk which had commenced. Superiority of the skies was an essential priority, never mind the small setbacks and the bigger efforts of token resistance.

The Luftwaffe in full strength beginning the onslaught in earnest determination. The question of keeping the youngsters in reserve for this corner was still being announced over the radio but there were no provisions to back this statement up. Another voice in the dessert, empty and void. The only thing to do for us was continuing our walk. We found Bredene bombed, every evening they told us, cross-roads the same story.

We found the region of Jan Baert, now French, still very Flemish, even Dunkirk and the hinterland it had only been ceded to the French in 1830 by the independence declaration of Belgium. Palmerston's Netherlands was never the same again once unity was lost, the new state would lose "Flandre du Nord", the left river side of the Schelde or Flemish Zealand and the Eastern Limburg supposed to put us off wanting independence, which was an advantage to the French speaking regions in the new Belgium because they gained greater representation in the Senate in Brussels. A very strange foreign package indeed! This is attributable to the Bishopry giving its blessing and alliance to that: excluding the House of Orange in one blow. This competition had been on since the middle ages among the two orthodox extremities.

The house of Orange against the Roman Catholic House of Tournai was a far cry from the landing of St. Wilibrod at Middlekerke who came to convert the Saxon Flemish and Dutch and St. Boniface who came to convert the Celtic Walloons and Germans of the Liege region. The House of Arras in turn exercised a greater influence on the southern region of Belgium.

North and South would keep their deep religious differences and would become immersed in them. To quote Erasmus the famous philosopher "Praise to Foolishness."

Nevertheless the south eventually would achieve a more liberalized spirit even at the turn of the century then we had to fight against various despotisms, even as before when we had to join forces with the Geuzen.

The Geuzen would from the waterways, the coastal regions helped by the House of Orange in Holland and by England to harass the Spaniards and those of similar beliefs.

Ostend was completely destroyed in this process and it took four years to accomplish the fact. It was said that Isabella the Infanta wouldn't change her shirt until that was done, hence the expression an Isabella shirt, meaning a dirty shirt.

The "Springers" Pole Vaulters, mostly from Friesian origin would be practically wiped out in that time, they would jump outside the walls over brooks and small streams at night cutting the throats and ears of the Spaniards and bringing the ears back for bounty.

Celts, Friesians, Franks, Saxons, Norse and Danes would leave their mark on the last of the Flemish by the previous invasions towards England, France and Ireland after the transition from Celts.

The Romanising would mainly take place in the south with the Walloons from which a different culture would evolve.

Shorter sporadic occupations would be ignored by both sides making it a Belgic question. Sometimes this trend would be marred by Walloon expansion. Holland or the Netherlands would be excluded, except for different general states we founded together with trade expansion during the East Indian era and American colonization. The aftermath of the "Battle of Waterloo, finished that off: also the unfair distribution by the officials of the United States of the Netherlands with jobs for their own, not by majority.

A short skirmish took place in Brussels and the bombardment of Antwerp eradicated any agreement by both sides for good.

It was rather Belgium then, more on the basis of the independence of the United States.

There was Dunkirk in all its splendor in front of us, all its old glory ready for total destruction. Some bombs had fallen here and there and people of all races were still roaming around the streets and sitting about looking at the passing refugees waiting for their ships to leave.

The first B.E.F. troops were also beginning to arrive. My Dad was always struggling and queueing for provisions to keep us on the go, and all of us couldn't have agreed more than to get out of this trap as quickly as possible, even if that meant before the evening. With our load still growing lighter every time we hurried off to the countryside on the back that would be the front facing the Germans now coming on the black horse.

By the fall of the evening we reached an old village called Chappelle-Saint-Pierre and found shelter in an opened school and looked after by French soldiers keeping order who accepted money bribes for inside boarding in the classrooms, so we slept outside. A Jewish family chasing and being given the inside. It would have been better if those soldiers had been at the front; maybe they were stragglers.

The battle of Dunkirk started in all earnestness to unfold in front of our eye, and we were like spectators in an amphitheater, sitting in that schoolyard on a blanket.

Goering was now sending his planes non-stop at night. We saw them swooping and diving in the searchlights. The continuous pounding of bombs and explosions of the anti- aircraft guns all intertwining continuously up in the sky as well as over the city making it a blazing inferno with fires and lightning; flashes of short outburst of fire with hick bellowing engulfing smoke. Sometimes we wondered about the planes coming to close for our comfort, but all glad we weren't there now and that we had followed our hunch.

The rumblings went on still further into the night but so tired had we become we just fell asleep on our straw mattresses. In the morning, after a quick bite and a drink, after our uneasy sleep saw us packing up once again in haste, the further away we could get in the shortest possible time from this doomed city the better.

Looking back in the morning sun we saw nothing else than huge columns of smoke rising up. "Think it all over", I told myself, "They might as well have given us all guns and rifles to fight back, we could be just as good as the soldiers".

Well for us Paris seemed to be more and more remote but we still struggled on relentlessly towards it. Of course, in this phony war we didn't know anything about Rommel busy cutting us off. Mind you it wouldn't take long, or it would be on us again, it looked like we were the only army trying to get somewhere. This grip was now taking shape and in proportion now, give us the weapons.

Eventually reaching for what I believed to be the old Paschendaele-Canal we found an empty barge that was able to take us at a price, further, it had no motor but a horse was ready to pull, at last we were going to save our poor feet.

Those plumb barges looked and moved like a long black dragon at a snail's pace through the still flat and cultivated countryside be speckled with well-kept and bigger farms than ours.
Our farms had never kept pace with the increasing population and lose of space.

Everything was in luster and bloom smelling of a good harvest. Sometime we walked alongside the horse, who came to know us very well. Keeping the same space between the coast, by day we could distantly see the long smoke funnels from Dunkirk,

This very same countryside had been every year frequented by our pickers, smallholders who came to do the beets here once upon a time. They were a special breed of hardy country people, not without swag bags. Working hard from early morning until late in the evening fulfilling their Sweethearts desires to set a home up.

They smoked their homegrown by themselves, bringing also a bit of life to the villages here. The beer was cheap, girls plentiful and all the old music of Breughel's feasting embodied in their dances and merrymaking with a gorging of the best farmers food. Our mouths were watering thinking of it. We were still not short of such as food and water in as much as they were supplying it.

When we called at farms they asked jokingly if we had come to bring in the harvest.   The general atmosphere was still friendly as before and the theatre of war somewhat removed from us, cordiality and innocence of the same events shared between us. The different characters who had taken the barge as their temporary floating home consisted of a variety of people one of whom was a lonely monk who didn't seem to belong to any particular group. The Monk was of course suspected of being a fifth columnist. This time they could have been right. He had a military countenance and could hardly converse with any of us, looked tall thin and pale and almost embodied the spirit of the epidemic which overtook Europe in the Dark Ages, followed by the pest, plague and starvation/even his attire took the shape of it. He disappeared suddenly in the night like the phantom of the Opera, in his cassock, collar and black case.

Afterwards the German vanguards would be much nearer than we thought. It looked like their ghost-figure had preceded them and forewarned us. It was very calm, to quiet before the storm. It seemed all too much like a bad omen. Indeed people were dying in mass around us now that was the prevailing feeling we had.

In St. Omalr the crossroads were heavily bombed and bombarded. That was the place we were heading for with reluctance.

Dunkirk was in flames and the drama of the beaches was unfolding itself behind us. Gravelines, Bologne and way up to Calais was just the same, Rommel busy hacking his way through and closing the gap, with the main body proceeding in France advancing relentlessly. Rumors, that later proved to be true, filtering through to us of a Scottish regiment hacked to pieces by S.S. troopers, near a little place called Paradis.

Those people were on their way back already, in other words everything looked pretty hopeless after this bad news. Right now we were in the process of watching an agile German spotter plane and its pilot trying to dodge a British fighter by playing the fallen leaf, right down to just over the treetops and getting away with it that was more than a sign and omen. They were here all around us, now for sure! The horse driver stopped, got paid off and packed up there and then to return as quickly as he could. Thus we were stuck and most people were leaving the barge and going in all directions.

The horse gave us a last farewell look in a despairing wind of way that only a horse can do and disappeared with its driver soon out of sight, to become just a small dot in the distance. It was finally just the skipper, family and us waiting for the following day and what might come with it? I think the Skipper was rather glad to have us as company.

The barge was our second home now; feeling lost in the depth of the hold and checking our luggage without the other people around we climbed back into the deck and indulged in a quiet talk, the calm waters gently lapping against the sides of the bulk of the flat nose of the boat, making us dwell on our own bewildered thinking when suddenly, as in a nightmarish dream and in magnitude only to be compared with the spectacle of Hieronymus, Bosch's renowned paintings of infamy and death's allegory, a whole display of them most unlikely planes in all history were passing by on different high and low altitudes hardly flying more like fluttering along in the sky southward bound. "The fly-past of decadence and corruption" This was the French Air Force in full strength. It was more like an apparition or maybe a mirage. No indeed shaking our heads in disbelief it was for real. Where was the Luftwaffe to catch the kites with a big net? Depressed we went to our bunks, there was no more hope for anything. The flight of incompetence I called it. Gloom and despair overcame us. Who was to blame for all those premeditated colossal blunders, the search for poor scapegoats had just begun, to cover up for all those bad shows. We heard all over by the allegory mad drunken crowd, "Nous Sommes Trakis" was the sudden cry which started with the infamous statesmen alike and was then picked up by the populace in rising crescendo. Probably some of those were flying in those kites by desperation because nobody of sound mind would have stepped in them.

Suddenly we heard that the Belgian king was the likely culprit and by preference his "Flemish People" a remark well taken, after all weren't we considered to be the "Boche du Nord." What were we supposed to do now, turn chicken like them, because they had never been able to push us around: that would have been a good enough reason? What an anachronism of a mind of sour grapes and no bravery to face up to facts. Now we knew too definitely where the road for us lay, straight back home, with the lions.

Meanwhile the B.E.F. was busy trying to get off the beaches with a few stragglers, permitted at the last minute, blowing a bridge up full with refugees, in a tactical retreat without any Germans being anywhere near. Considering British stiff upper lip policy, they seemed just as panicky under strain as the rest of humanity. Little did they knew that crazy Hitler had let them leave the beaches with their little boats so that he could tell how he had beaten them, to the full amazement of his own generals who already had their guns in place for the final assault and encirclement.

The planes only kept pinpricking those most of the bombs getting muffled in the sand. The strafing was the worst on the long columns standing or wading in queues like sitting ducks. Surely the whole "Luftwaffe" was not used on those points otherwise it would have been a total massacre. Hitler seemed to have a knack for doing things that way, which eventually made him our best lunatic at large, and for the Germans their worst enemy. This would help greatly to shorten the holocaust. Otherwise it would have been worse for everybody. We had to work on our own strategy to cope with this and find a way to our best advantage.

To begin with early in the morning we explored the other bank with high thick trees. I believe that gave some protection from the air. The Skipper helped us to take our cases to the side in his little boat, "a skipperschiuite" and we said farewell to the nice fellow that he was, tears in our eyes, and waving goodbye to his family. My Father warning him that he shouldn't stay on the boat.

We had just placed our cases down, when a dogfight started above us, planes diving after each other, the big bullets cascading and ricocheting amongst us, we kept the trees between them and ourselves as a shield. Our yellow blankets were on again, ideal targets, looking like French soldiers I think, carrying ammunition which the cases would like to Spotters and Gunners from a distance. We had not gone two paces further after the dog fight when suddenly as from nowhere but really from the direction of St. Omaire appeared a low flying spotter plane above the treetops which was clearly visible to us the instant we looked up, grey green fuselage with black crosses on the wings and the red Swastika at an angle on the rudder. Well there you were, right in it, could it be plainer than that.

More refugees coming back in hast and hysterical panic with grim stories of shootings, bayoneting;   and with the victims hanging on the barbed wire fences hacked to pieces. The only thing left for us to do was to make for the open fields in front of us: if we kept to the road following the canal the troopers would be quicker after us as there was no resistance anywhere. Trying to get as much distance in the shortest time between the last point near the barge and the length of the field with a drain ditch between us we covered a couple of kilometers, when suddenly we heard the short sharp speedy droning of two low flying Dornier's from the direction of St. Omair skimming over the canal between the lane of trees and the place where we had left the barge, releasing their bombs in quick succession. Witnessing what followed, the barge, what was left of it, went up in broken and splintered planks, boards flying in all directions. We hoped the Skipper had heeded the warning for him and his family. There was no time to turn back or wonder what we could have done as we suddenly came under fire ourselves. The German Artillery had us in its sights and smells began falling short of us only twenty yards away. Before we could hear more of the distant deep sounding bangs of the guns and the whistling shells following us we quickly dived in the ditch and continued at a rapid pace following the ditch till we were safely behind a big farm wall.

No doubt they had taken us for soldiers and once out of sight they had lost us and didn't waste any more ammunition. How close it had been!

A toothless old crow appeared from the old farmstead mumbling it was an English exercise and not to worry about it. The old lady, as she looked more like a witch should have looked, should have looked a bit better in her crystal ball we thought, and we left her where she stood as we all turned around and saw a few more craters opening up on her land. Maybe the German gunners thought that was a couple more to prove to the contrary. The old woman went back inside in some doubt.

As we didn't fancy being stuck there we hurried along until we reached the bend in the winding curving road facing the other way again taking our steps North once more, coming to another canal behind a little village called Bergues, derived from the Flemish Bergen for mountains, more like little hills, as that is what they appeared to be.

A British platoon was busy behind Bergues and the canal working to enlarge and digging their trenches very close to the bridge. They were all nice chaps and we thought just the same after the adverse news not to go over that bridge with the Hun so near so we started a nice conversation calmly telling what we had seen with the German's on the back of us, to close for comfort, from where we had come.

A scout was sent straight away on a motor-bike in that direction and it didn't take long for him to return and verify the statement. The only course left to them was to retreat swiftly and leave the trenches as they were before being cut off, now we hoped for their success in a tactical retreat as it came so often to be called. Maybe we could have been left with the fighting to do and all. No weapons and half-finished trenches to bury oneself in.

The ghost of the Duke must have been having a hell of a time observing all this. All the battles that have been waged here with so many armies of nations, dignitaries and Generals all blessed with the same holy waters. The victims rotting in Flanders earth with their blood fertilizing the soil. "To each his own".

We were under continuous scrutiny in this phony war as never before, faced as we were with just being the spectators for a short time. Friendship only seems to be skin deep fighting was an individual thing between the various forces so a stable front was never achieved.

It was fractional and broken up nobody to fill the gaps or even to get the chestnuts out of the fire, everybody for himself. The only achievement here and there, a passive resistance and covering up rear action.

As the platoon was soon out of sight we continued our march towards Hondschote and the border again where we crossed into Belgium and we felt just like victorious warriors of "The Battle of the Golden Spurs", who kissed the ground before going into battle, we were so glad to be back on home ground.

We had been insulted, not given bread or water anymore since those silly remarks by irresponsible Statesmen, even by our distant cousins in those territories that were French now. We couldn't forget or forgive any of them either, not at the moment. The hurt had cut deep; cowardice and subservience were not our weaknesses at any time: lest we forget. Once wrongly challenged our wrath would have to be reckoned with.

Once in Belgium the place was still pretty full of German hordes and other foreign troops for that matter. Thank goodness for that breathing space. Babbling brooks to dangle our tired and blistered feet in, food and water plenty. A small British garrison was still left behind on a farm and a friendly soldier offered us some bully-beef.

Before any of us could answer, my Grandmother gave an absolute "no". He probably wondered what it was all about! The feeling would take some time to go away from the previous bad confrontation we had had, considering that we were anglophiles.

If a bigger nation like France had to be placated by British politicians, then we thought certainly they had to put up with their own chicanery also. Don't expect us to do the dirty work, unless we are respected and part of the same setup, freely, and we would prove our worth. Anyway the farmer looked after us very well, we ate at the same table as in days gone by, we had always been known for this kind of hospitality, it was an honor to accommodate the stranger in your home and land. This was about the end of that custom because at the end of the war there was no such thing anymore. The rat race had begun, anything else is tantamount to softness. No more code of honor or hospitality to keep.

The first long and sound sleep soon engulfed our tired minds and bodies.

After a good breakfast of eggs and boerespek, "Gammon" instead of the weak bowl of coffee with crusts in France that had been introduced, we felt ourselves more rejuvenated again. Some of the soldiers we were watching were very young, near the wagon-train waiting for food, when suddenly out of nowhere over the treetops again a low flying Dornier came on the scene making them run and jump like rabbits among the cabbages.

Luckily it was too sudden and the pilot hadn't observed any of them or had been ready, maybe he just let them be. Their rifles were standing like tripods when they came back with embarrassment showing on their faces.

The very same way I felt near Bredune from the De Panne trip, that day when my Dad told me off. They weren't told off. Everybody goes through the same frustrations and trials, baptism by fire, soldiers and civilians all alike. This was' more than any other war Like that, as civilians became more vulnerable from the beginning of the hostilities due to the intimidation.

Psychology was applied now. Propaganda by the religious front, business and politics lost impetus among the Western populations and became concentrated on the underdeveloped nations falling on gullible ears. For how long?

Leaving this last development behind us we headed Surefooted for the coast again at an angle towards the North Sea.

Reaching the white sand dunes across the nearby fertile polder ground, away from the bulk of the incoming enemy assembling somewhere for the final push or say rather walk over, we may say so now. The dunes in straight line either way also made and formed better protection against bombs as a good deal of the blast got muffled up; one could hide better and look out over the flatland for an approaching enemy, by land air or even sea, which was expected at any minute. Shelter everywhere with occasional visits to the farms, we felt very free for the time being in this last bit of open strip and corner. If nobody had the foresight to use it we at least did.

The tram stations along the coastal strip had all been destroyed. Our first real hold up was in front of Newport, when we arrived in the evening at a big farm, as we had to leave our dunes to swerve around the town to reach the harbor.

Belgian soldiers already installed on the farm and in defensive positions made room for us sharing their meagre rations, telling us that this was likely to be their last bit, according to the news, as both our allies had fled, they made a last stand on the spot more for Newport than Dunkrirk.

We tried to sleep afterwards, we could hear them telling about the intense battles and skirmishes during their retreat, in subdued voices, they had passed through, from the beginning with so many comrades wounded and lost without much purpose in all. The wages of war I suppose.

We fell asleep to the murmur of their voices. After a short breakfast we gathered ourselves together to brace the last kilometers. Not without the soldiers warning that the Stuka bombers came regularly at 7 o'clock in the morning to bomb around the bridge, at the other side of Newport and near the harbor.
With this message we thanked them and left, we got through the town safely, very much deserted like everywhere.

When we reached the bridge we noticed everything around was very much in ruins and destroyed except the bridge itself, with a Belgian soldier in front of it and small shelter for him.

One soldier with a rifle to protect and defend the bridge, the town, the harbor and the sluices on this side west, the Germans would reach from North and East. His bridge was saved by the Stuka's by the look of it, for the German army, the Stuka's terrorized anybody around or approaching the bridge.

As we were pondering on this, and him positively verifying the Stuka's attacks came regular as clockwork. We could hear the Stuka's droning in the distance more heavily as German planes hid behind some roundish cloud formations still near the horizon. "That's them" he said now making ready to get in his shelter, you had better do the same.

The dreaded sound was steadily approaching till the small specks started taking shape in the sky and heading straight for us in the reflection of the sunlight.

They started spreading out and stretching their flight like eagles ready for their dives: picking their respective targets out from high above.

42

For a moment I thought we were a bit to visible to make a run for it. It was time to take evasive action and scatter but where? There was not enough room in the shelter!

My Grandmother was already halfway across the bridge but we didn't find that very wise to follow. My Mother and I ran back towards the ruins and lay flat behind a wall from where we saw the first plane do its low trial run.

My Dad screaming to come back: to what? Too late anyway and him jumping in the shelter as the first bombs started to come down. In between them we jumped up and made for the first cellar we saw further away and across facing us, already full with the inhabitants and neighbors. Extra room was made for us.

Now the shrieking of the Stuka's and screaming bombs started in earnest, our little shelter shuddering and wobbling like a jelly.

Possibly it was only for ten minutes but for us it was like a life time. Meanwhile everybody was wondering what was happening to the others who weren't there.
When it was all over and we heard the planes gradually fading away, we climbed out dazed by the smoke and dust observing the sun through this screen looking like a scene of the end of the world.

Thanking God and the people, proceeding towards the bridge we could now see, as the air had cleared. My dad and the soldier just rising out of this compact hole as it was with a cover on top and sides made of sandbags piled on top and around still rubbing their eyes, not believing their luck and again the bridge intact, honestly they couldn't have possibly have missed it even if they wanted to.

No trace of my Grandmother. We thought the worse now, what may have happened to her. My Dad saying some shrapnel of a brisant bomb had just missed him while he was shouting at us and diving for cover head over tail into the shelter. Everything seemed to be still there, as far as we could see, the same as before.

I noticed the soldier had also a machine gun now, maybe that's what I had heard short bursts, I hoped that my Grandmother was safe, he couldn't have shot her by mistake, surely.

After this we quickly crossed the bridge and noticed my Grandmother appearing like a banshee from under a previously burned and shelled skeleton of an army car: swearing and cursing, waving her arms in anger at the disappearing flying machines, she should have had a machine gun!

To stay here any longer was asking for a repeat performance, so we gathered our wits together and took a last look at the monument of King Albert which had been slightly touched by shrapnel and had been part of the shelter with the army vehicle close by. It turned out to be a good shelter after all but you never know, listening to the droning and feeling the vibrations all around us. We also saw the sluices opened by the brave sluice guard that had let the waters through. The fishing hangers seemed to have had a good few bombs, also the sheds and boats. Now it was time to proceed on our march back, for us, following close to the ditches along the highway.

Heading straight for the sands and our for certain safe passage off the beaten track. Soon we came to Westende and Middelkerke and were on home ground. From here we saw German Dorniers deliberately bombing a convent with the red crosses clearly visible for miles around. What a cruel thing to do, what was Goering and his henchmen up to.

We were tired and fed-up with these silly war games and didn't know what to expect in Ostend. The war was not even over.

We decided to call in on my Mum's sister in Wilskerke, Elisa, which was not too far off just veering a bit off inland towards the polder. Just as well as it turned out later.

We turned off at St. Willibrod's Church still called after him in Middlekerk and arrived in no time at my Aunt Elisa's safe house, I should say, everybody glad to see each other. What a surprise they never had left of course. Wise people they were unless you wished to be blasted away, it was best to stay. Everything seemed to be on its last legs now and they said we might as well stay till then, who knows what was still in store with such an unscrupulous adversary to cope with.

Hun, German what was the difference. Both their war like intentions had been known since time immemorial. Our welcome was warm and cordial and that was the main thing, everybody was glad to see the other one intact. My Uncle Odiel had made a little shelter that could take us all,   in the fields a good way away from the house.

As evening was setting, we could see Ostend in the distance straight over the openness of the windswept prairies, that's what they looked like. Similar to Dunkirk it was covered in smoke burning all over with fires everywhere, we could hear the pounding of the incessant bombing, planes flying away and coming back relentlessly with another load. Nothing was over yet and with so many souls expiring as we sensed by this useless slaughter we thought it better to get to the shelter in time.

The Mother of my Uncle sat with her Alsatian dog which was very nervous sensing the atmosphere, the lady religiously declaring this was the anti-Christ at work, and we ourselves felt that we had had a bellyful of everything.

We were held in the grip of the last moments, it was intense and you could feel the tension also, but we were all together. A consolation somehow against the terror of what might be in store together with a feeling of utter desolation pressing down on us.

This was the intention of the enemy to take the last spiritual resistance away for his own cruel inner sadistic satisfaction.

The heaviest of this punishment was poured out on the so called Jewish quarters, the nice Chapel Street, and the huge hotels on the dike full up with wounded soldiers, the docks and workers quarters. What a kiss of death, the Casino went to.

The fires on the wood docks were tremendous and lit up the evening sky, they illuminated the targets perfectly. A couple of planes dropped their loads near us, an old German shelter called the "dronkenpit" because of the way it was tilted by a delayed explosive: giving one the impression of feeling drunk while walking down the spiraling stairway. The dike near us had also received bombs and a Belgian horse team had been decapitated,

As all shops were closed, the following morning saw my Dad and Uncle deciding to use the opportunity to stock the larder up against more shortages and both went and cut steaks from the fresh killed horses as nobody objected. It didn't take them long and they returned like hunters with their dripping slabs of fresh meat.

The big news brought back was that the British Fleet, mostly destroyers, was laying in front of the coast at a close distance watching; and any minute a fierce dual between the advancing German forces and the fleet was expected, with us in between. So quickly back into the shelter after distributing the meat with no hanky-panky.

The confrontation would be terrible, just imagine the size of those guns, and keep on praying.

After a while of unusual quietness nothing seemed to be happening after great expectations: the real fighting was over. Secret agreement, stalemate, whatsoever, we were safe. An unspoken presence of just in case, you don't touch me, I will let you alone too. A silent non-aggression pact. As long as most of the little boats out of view here got free from the beaches unscathed.

Not long after we reappeared like groundhogs from the flimsy hole and the holocaust of fire that could have been unleashed. We will never know how close it all was, thank goodness.
One likes his country, his city his people subconsciously but when something happens tantamount to a catastrophe of certain and horrible proportions then it stays imprinted on his mind forever. There is not much left to one's imagination.

The German grey coated columns kept moving along behind us keeping to the canal of Passchendile under cover of the trees towards the sea. Endless columns just like 1914-18 when some people remarked they must be going in circles to produce such lengthy amounts of robot-like soldiers keeping on continuously. One must remember the size of Belgium against the bigger surrounding nations. Belgium is only double the size of Ulster, Northern Ireland.

The eighteenth day battle campaign was about to come to an infamous end and again as Julius Caesar in his chronicles about the Belgic tribes in Northern Gaul, said he encountered the most resistance; at least he was telling the truth.

King Leopold III in the old castle near Tourhout left behind by his Government, already gone into exile, made a statement that he would rather stay with his people who didn't seem to care one way or the other. He waited to capitulate until the last soldier of the allied forces

46

had left the beaches, meanwhile the Germans were still bombing Ostend.

An artillery of articulated guns had taken up position next to us, starting to give regular salvos at the soldiers near Newport.

I suppose our King thought it was better to give up than complete annihilation. He had kept his side of the bargain except for going to England to continue the struggle and that was a grave mistake, he would have to abdicate on this in dishonor and being ignored for all the rest. As far as we were concerned, still in our little shelter expecting the worse to happen, it was a relief on hearing the news of capitulation in one way and at the same time apprehensive as to what it would entail.

Running to the house we now saw the Germans passing by in their vehicles: it had started to drizzle now, the sunshine was gone both ways and gaiety with it, somber, grinning faces especially one on the motor bike, looking at us pompous with victory. What a specter to envisage for the coming years.

Staying with his people the whole Royal family spent sunny holidays in the south of Franco's Spain where Baldouin would meet his Fabiola and "Us" his people were in for the dark years of despair in camps or starvation. I don't know what his immediate circles had to do with this and what influenced him, this was an un-pleasant fact with further developments in the offing.

There was no end to the gossip and rumors as to what and why? Unpopular it proved to be and would stay so. That it was treason, far from that; it just was a bad move not to go into exile, because that is where the battle could be won or continued.

Capitulation and occupation were just other names for his people being overrun anyway, perhaps we would have experienced worse treatment afterwards too bad to contemplate. For most of us it couldn't have been worse anyway. There was of course a great possibility all due to a bit of bad propaganda.

The Germans would like that too, and do their best to fan it up. All Hitler's deeds go for everybody concerned as they all suited themselves. Later he did it to his own people. We can speculate who he liked best; nobody I suppose. Kill them all, starting with the most likely ones, that's how it turned out.

Big gun carriers, filled to the brim with soldiers were temporarily parked close to us, waiting for orders and one of the young bullies dropped his bayonet at my Dad's feet and I watched with trepidation, that could be the start of a massacre, depending on how my Dad reacted.

I knew all of his stories from the first World War, I knew of his courage but also of his common sense: looking at us and smiling he picked the damned thing up as if it was hot and presenting it back to front like a non-aggression offering he gave it back to the soldier. Which was accepted with a short snappy "danke".

We gave a relieved sigh and thought what a close shave that had been.

All of us were breeding secret thoughts of how to get this well armed enemy just the same, we had to use underhanded methods from now on. Far too many and all that material it was rather difficult to try and jump them as had been done in the past with success. We had to bide our time. It is no good to be a dead soldier or single hero, this was not the day for martyrdom. The battle was over for us for a while. We had our horse steaks to deal with and did not wish to deplete the supplies of our helpful Aunt. The hearty meal carried us further on our way towards Ostend which we were finally able to reach to be met by a shambles of immense proportions.

The last minute bombing had left its destruction path in our wake, craters and debris all over the place. Telephone poles and lights in all positions laying across the streets. Some people walking aimlessly around with an incomprehensible glazed look.

On reaching the center cross roads called "Petit Paris" people told us Hitler Youth had stood on the corners of an enormous swastika flag, spread out trying to engage the attention of the German planes who were still bombing with their troops already crossing the town.

Approaching the Chapel Street that was practically destroyed, people were still coming from the dyke after helping rescue the wounded out of the hotels, they had gruesome tales to tell. The Casino was destroyed also. The British ships lay in front, with the German artillery firing a couple of shots, quickly ordered by the officers to stop and proceed immediately towards France.

The same stories we heard from the few witnesses all over, most of the population being in the shelters at the time. The great storm had subsided and calmed down.

It was a great time to take account of it all. After this we proceeded in safety crossing the bridge as usual, intact and continued to the old tram station where we had started our trip to near Bourbourg and back on the road to Saint-Omaire. We looked back in utter disbelief at the backlash and eagerness to totally bombing of Ostand on the mad orders given by their leaders, similar to the destruction of Rotterdam.

The first German motorized platoon was completely annihilated, plastered on both sides of the house walls on the curve of the entrance to Ostend, its own soldiers crucified by their own planes. Most of the evidence had been quickly taken away such as the bodies and human remnants but the wrecks of cars and the blood spattered all around was overwhelming. I wondered how the communique would be worded, describing the event about those heroes fallen in battle, to the parents, wives and children.

Would it be described as one of the hazards of war, fallen in the line of duty to the Fatherland on foreign soil.

I don't think anybody enjoyed that either on any side and therefore we are back to each his own.

Where was the victory in all of this? Luckily we were on our own, finding our way throughout the useless debris, otherwise we could have been mistaken for looters. The big ramp with busts of opulent women set in bronze, one saved and intact, it crossed the rail-track and sluices from the Barquentine station towards the wood docks and onwards to Brussels. This was an enterprise started in the reign of Leopold II. The pious fathers of the Bishopry had to interfere with this project with the pretense that their flock needed protection from the nakedness, the ladies displayed had to be removed under indignant protest. Maybe the Germans would have used them for their shells anyway! Cannon fodder.

All this was a travesty of free thought and liberal ideas the country had been used to for centuries, its arts, culture and progressive policies.

It also became the cornerstone that would help to tumble the empires around us, examples and ideas that would flow from it and the rescue of many exiles from oppression.

On the right of me I looked upon the Maria Hendrika Park or what was left of it that contained the covered casemates of the Spanish occupation 1601 - 1605 at the siege of Ostend.

Maria Hendrika was the dowager who preferred to live in Belgium and so took up residence. Franz Joseph was obliged to leave Belgium because of the revolt of the "Boerenkrijg", another Boer-War, despite his many reforms.

Napoleon Bonaparte another occupier was responsible for building a fort in the dunes: which was strategically placed to protect the harbor and on the other side of the town which we had just entered from Middlekerke the old Fort-Wellington only a frontage left.

The Guilds had played the biggest part in defending our freedoms to get our "Charters" established sometimes in support of aristocratic families, Counts, Barons, Bishops of Liege or The Counts of Flanders, offspring of Arthacanute and Robrecht de Frisian.

The "Pax Romana" with the Spanish after their infamous fury was over provided a renaissance and the return of famous people like Pieter Paul Rubens who became Ambassador for the King. Trade began to flourish including that, with the New World. Our new Governors Albrecht and Isabella would become the intermediaries and pacifiers.

The Flemish fleet would never recover its formal glory but the cruel times of the terrible Alva were over and his inquisitors, burning heretics, plundering and destroying were finished. The best of the fleet stayed in Holland and so did the East Indian Company, founded in Ostend.

The Black Death and starvation played its part after the religious wars were over and Bruges lost its outlet to the sea by neglect.

From our vintage point it was a short time before we noticed the marine school had been partly destroyed by a "Voltreffer", as they called it, a direct hit. The body of one of my school friends was still in it which we later came to know, was the reason for him being missing. He had gone there to get himself a typewriter at the crucial moment the bombing took place, his one and only ambition in life to be a reporter, his life cut short in one moment attempting to achieve his ambition.

It was really looting, considering it was our tax-payers money getting lost and destroyed; only to be thieved over again by the invader against our legal status, from defender of our own innocent country in the different conflicts we found ourselves involved every time by no fault of our own.

Germany as a bigger nation was forcing us to give a passageway to be able to strike at the other nations. This was nothing new but rape of the innocent bystander, it was at war with. After this we passed the Tilbury Dock well known by John Coceralls ships trading with England such goods as Danish bacon and all kinds of southern fruits corning in from Italy, Spain etc.

On the other side the endless smoldering and in many places burning of numerous wood piles recently brought in by the Scandinavian boats, stored for further transportation inland and abroad. Our homecoming was quite a spectacle.

I noticed my tree was still there and so was the house, there were many gaps where other houses had originally stood and on the other side of the creek well, it looked more like a mouth with broken teeth than a row of houses. Some of our best friends were killed in the bombing. A foul smell of humans mixed with plaster and wood was hanging over those places, especially with the present dampness from rainy weather.

Complete families had disappeared in one swoop from the direct hits "voltreffers" such people as the Swanepoels and Krugers; in the wages of war.

Our throats and mouths were so dry and we had looked forward to quenching our thirsts with some of the old stocks my grandmother had in her beer cellar, saved for years for such an occasion. Good old fashioned beers matured to perfection called Guzen-Lambic beer. We would now indulge before the Germans could lay their hands on it, what a lovely thought; this turned out to be an idle dream and the biggest disappointment yet of the whole trip, we were now at the cursing stage.

Our neighbors thinking their moment had come during the bombing had drunk themselves into oblivion. This must have been going on since our departure.

Anyway some had a good time in bad circumstances and made the best of it, right now some were busy stocking their larders with all the bully beef, nestle milk and boxes filled with all kinds of tinned food left behind in the dockyards by the B. E. F.

By the time we had reestablished ourselves in the house the Germans had put their guards on the places and we managed just about to rummage a couple of boxes that was to last for the duration of the war; we were done for.

You had to be glad with better than next to nothing from now on, if you didn't want to get shot in the process.

The Germans claimed it as their booty and we were the looters now, there was not much change for filling our larders anymore.
The propaganda press and tourists came to take pictures of the devastation their bombs had caused, the bodies of the victims rotting away underneath. We heard that one member of the Kruger family had survived, his knocking had been heard and he had been pulled from the rubble but his mind had gone, poor fellow. He was the oldest uncle of the children who I knew so well. "Rix" and I had been astonished at the daring things he did to the eldest Rix to enjoy just before the war got on its way. He seemed to get the last kick out of living as if he knew time was running short for him.

The queues for the tinned food came to definite stop with the German officers disciplining their soldiers for being too soft on us. Now and again gun shots were fired in the air to let us know who was in charge.

The following six months was without shortages but once the restriction orders came into force it hit us badly. The occupation forces wanted everything for themselves even sending things to Germany and on top of that we had the blockade to contend with, this resulted in the farmers hiding their harvest for themselves and the black market.

With almost total restriction movement it would be increasingly difficult to get some food in. The rationing was abysmal and you could hardly live on it. Not only was it meagre but the quantity and quality was just about at survival level from starvation.

In those days and before big columns of prisoners passed our door, going towards Germany guarded by a few Germans.

Some of the Belgians ran away and hid till they could go home under the amnesty which was given after six months which Hitler provided for the Flemish soldiers. Maybe he hoped with this adverse news to sow dissention and put a wedge between the unity which was already shaky. It was fully used and they went home, most of them to form the resistance movement. People who denied their Flemish roots to take the French side were only too glad to revert back to their origins to take advantage of the amnesty: some Walloons were also glad to take advantage of the situation after previous claims to have no knowledge of Flemish.

My Grandmother also remembered the bad treatment we had received from the French soldiers, no water or food, so it was tit for tat as far as she was concerned, short of spitting them in the face.

What happens to one is bound to happen to the other, all this has been said by famous philosophers like Erasmus and many others just to note Erasmus's "Praise to Foolishness" for a beginning.

The old lady would hold to her position on this stand after being snubbed and I know quite a few others felt the same, like General De Gaulle and Mrs. Baels family. Lillian Baels was the second wife of King Leopold the third, They had all experienced the same attitude and everybody had ended up in snubbing each other, of course the natural reaction to this was easier for some to get over than others, only time will heal the bitterness it created as long as it doesn't go the other way.

We had to forgive and forget in order to keep our heads, after a while petty thinking was out. The battle to better was better than to give in to worse situations.

It was time to collect our wits and train in the lull. Weapons that had been thrown away were retrieved and cleaned, oiled and then hidden away again. We gave ourselves a rough going over, hardening our bodies like the Spartans, also living like it, on that we had no choice. All the tricks of unarmed combat were learned with the help of the additional operatives who had been parachuted in. I don't think there was much the Special Forces could have taught us in all of this, except their own codes and systems with contacts which was picked up by our teachers anyway.

The harassing of the enemy took all forms and shapes on a day to day basis from helping ourselves to ration cards in the offices, to changing passes, obtaining provisions, stripping abandoned or requisitioned buildings and general acts of sabotage. Schools were closed or used by the military and when they reopened much later there wasn't very much available in the way of supplies: most of us used the trade schools as they were giving extra rations of sardines there, also you could wait to take your final examinations, because they wanted skilled youngsters to send to their factories in Germany, also becoming short of people.

If you didn't go it was forced labor for you so we had to prepare ourselves well before this, and make our own plans which was only for those who dared. During the six months pause I managed to get myself a small skipper's boat which I had noticed laying half submerged and tied to a barge in the wood docks. A bomb had sunk the barge and I figured the "schuite" a skipper's boat to be pretty well intact and worth the effort. We asked the sluice guard if we could have it and he agreed, considering it to be war booty for us, otherwise it would rot away and the Germans had no interest in it anyway.

The whole contraption was held by a thick rope from the top of the quay by me, with some help, and I had the idea to get a sharp bread knife worked into a polo stick I had at an angle and hook it around the very thick rope of the connection to both boats, once that was done an up and down movement in the water would gradually cut the rope at the same time my old school friend "Achiles" was holding the grappled schuite so as not to lose it and I joined in helping him secure the boat. The whole operation took less than ten minutes and was so successful we couldn't believe our own eyes. Having the schuite freed we pulled it to the bridge between the two docks which turned out to be a considerable distance away. Ducking under the bridge we had to maneuver and continue along the whole length of the next dock till we found a ramp to pull it upon, the problem now was to get to the creek.

This had taken a good deal of the day so one of us had to stand guard till the next morning while the others looked for a cart big enough to transport the vessel in.

My Dad found an old customer of my Grandmother, a caretaker of the Tilbury Dock and sheds and he got us the best cart available, with all hands now getting the boat on it on the small wharf near the Billard & Creighton works who were trawler makers.

Once this was achieved it was quite easy to pull and push it to the creek to put it on the grassy slope close to the Ibis, a boarding school for seaman's orphans. The shrapnel damage on the side we managed to mend with a plank from the wood piles and caulked the rest to make it watertight and it was as good as ever.

From the bombed and burned out Tilbury offices we procured a flagpole for a mast, sail and canvas we got from the cellar, it had been used to cover the boiler.

The two oars were another matter, we procured two straight stems from the spars on the inland sand dunes the remains of a wooded area which soon completely disappear. I wouldn't say by encroaching civilization but rather by unscrupulous stripping mostly by the occupier. The only trouble not being a hardwood they would bend slightly so we fixed it by putting sleds on and bolting the planks in between.

The day of the launching was approaching and all old friends and neighbors were present. It was the Vikings again going out a roving: after this the creek, the river North-Ede to Bruges and front harbor were never safe again while it lasted. We sailed, tackled, trawled and rowed to our hearts content, argued when one pulled too much to one side especially the very strong one called Gentils against the weakest of the group in athletics called Pierre so that the boat would go in a spin when they were aboard but everybody had a good time.

We augmented our food supply with eels, flat fish and sea bass, we also cultivated mussel beds and were thinking of going out to sea just in front of the coast, that is the amount of leeway we were allowed because we were under close surveillance, but who knows was the hope, a sudden mist and we might have been able to get away. A couple had succeeded to do just that but only made it, the other never survived the strafing that followed soon after. After a while one could not even get onto the beaches there was barbed wire everywhere plus mines and guns pointed at you.

My Dad kept away from the boat; one day he got caught by his own rod which had a double hanger with hooks to fish with, on one side, as he tried to reel in a wiggling eel, it managed to swing wildly and the other hook embedded in his right cheek.

I don't know who was catching who but it was another thing to free him from the entanglement.

All good things had to come to an end now, one day Achiles and I having finished collecting the ropes from the barquentine, which had been thrown in before the Government left for England, were involved in an Incident that knocked me head first into the water: I was hauling in the ropes at great speed and Achile was rowing, unfortunately he wasn't looking where he was going and we headed straight into the rear of a bigger boat and as I was standing upright the upper rear end of the barge knocked me over into the water which was none to warm and I had to swim to the boat which was heavy going as I was fully clothed, shoes and all.

To keep warm we rowed as fast we could and we were still fiercely arguing as we passed the Tilbury wharfs that were being used for loading German Torpedoes on to speed boats, the German sailors watching us too closely thought the worst and somehow knocked their delicate load.   An unexpected chain reaction started gradually developing from that and transferring to everything else like a slow running fire, all I knew was that sparks started to fly suddenly in all directions, what had happened I'll never know and we suddenly found ourselves rowing for dear life while the spattering of ammunition increased behind us from small explosions to a whole battery of bullets going off simultaneously, it was like being on a battleground.

We just made it towards the stairs opposite our house, after securing the boat, then the whole wharf seemed to rise up in a great glowing red flame as we looked back and waited for the deafening bang which we knew would result from the explosions.

When the displacement of air came we were blown along by the force and sled sideways into the hallway and quickly descended into the cellar for shelter.   Before our dash for safety we noticed a cyclist coming towards us, who never had to pedal, he was just swept away with the force of the rushing wind which carried him along for kilometers he later told us.

We never could figure out how this thing had really started. A busload of German artists and tourists dispatched to the war zone for entertainment had waited too long on the signals, before the last man came rushing through the fence to tell them to get away in a hurry and run, which they did after first receiving the full blast in their faces bleeding profusely from the cuts on their heads.

Afterwards we took a little walk further on from the scene wondering what else might go up and met up with the cyclist who told us about the free and effortless ride he had made.

After it was all over and quiet we went back and could find no trace of the sailors, laborers or flack team on a tower who were watching the whole incident in their last doomed moments, unbeknown to them.

Soon afterwards a detachment of officers and soldiers made a thorough house search in our row or "wyk", bayonets on rifles, luger drawn in hand pointed towards us; as they looked at my dad's recommendation on the wall picturing Belgian soldiers with rifle and bayonet looking at them too wearing the Yzer Cross on the Yzer front of 1914-1918. I thought, now we are in for it especially with the rifle pointed at them for their father's deeds.

A few questions were asked, and I understood with our low German Flemish dialect, about whether we had seen a couple of fellows with a boat who had been near the scene about the time of the explosion. Of course that is the bit we didn't or couldn't understand, we kept our fingers crossed. Phew that was close! The carelessness of the German sailors turned the catastrophe to our favor far better than any sabotage could have done at that moment in time and that is how it was. I remember also on a bicycle trip with my friend Achiles, along grounds used for maneuvers, looking at a biplane shortly before hostilities started;

Before the war the Belgians practiced shooting at an exercise bag pulled by another bi-plane near a little place called Le Cocq, I heard my friend Achilles say: I wish that the plane would fly into the bag. And it did! The pilot parachuted out and was rescued, after it happened he remarked to himself; full of remorse, I am sorry; I didn't mean that; Maybe it was premonition, for the arsenal we didn't feel the least pity; this was war for us and nothing else mattered when hostilities commenced.

The last days were coming rapidly to a close. Soon the little boats had to be tied up in an enclosed protected small dock. I never saw my boat again: afterwards my Dad gave my Uncle the papers and a similar one was sold after hostilities, I do not think it was mine although I could have recognized it, but I was to busy recuperating after the war to investigate. Somebody made a good deal somewhere.

The area was flooded with German ferrets asking all kinds of questions and opinions, with the barges with their fronts cut off to allow vehicles to be taken on board from the installations along the banks were appearing everywhere, to take on the military paraphernalia, provided it was not too big.

All peace and quiet had gone and our allies the British had to bomb all this in return without choice and we would be in the midst of it again. I think we had more than enough of it and moved away into town where we got bombed instead as a convoy moved throughout and an articulated gun was chased by the flyer, also to remember the bombs that most of the time missed hitting the flack team nearest and above us which was placed on an old hotel called the Canon Hotel, eventually they blasted them out of the position on the rooftop into oblivion.

We thought it safer to have a ride to the countryside and a stricken plane proceed to drop its bombs right next to us in a field. We just couldn't win.

For a time no matter where we went the bombing was following us. We decided to take a rest with an old aunt of my Dad's in Beerst near Diksrruide, and that was alright for a while. Enough to eat there and we could still take long rides into the surrounding countryside and look for apples and vegetables.

Slowly our funds where running out and my Dad had to go back to town to live, with us following him. Restrictions where really biting and hard to bear now with the end of the war nowhere in sight. We were placed in good homes from Doctor friends my Mother knew very well, but the Germans requisitioned it all in turn, even my bike, as soon as we became nicely settled in.

I hid in the trade schools where most resistance and information was gathered and given out from there too. I was offered the chance to join, somebody put my name straight on a list which was the last straw as I thought that an unwise thing to do, fancy giving the enemy a chance to get at you through a list, so I didn't join. Many were caught this way and one of my friends even lost his head because of his patriotic fervor when he was captured and spit in their faces. This was too simple an action and not for me to be extinguished. I had another turn in the countryside with another good aunt on my Mother's side near the border, so I had the opportunity to study the possibilities for making a crossing near there, it was pretty easy for the daring again.

Total starvation was relieved on the coastal region by miraculous events such as all the herring and sprats becoming stuck near Dunkirk and Calais, backing right up to Ostend.

The little boats which were still allowed to catch them, came in loaded to the brim and near to the danger point of sinking through the sheer weight of the catch.

We ate herring morning, noon and night, exchanged them for food with the farmers, which we smuggled in from the countryside to keep ourselves and boxers alive for the sake of sport, the only entertainment available which came to the peak of revival.

It was a shame the German propaganda got hold of them to elevate Flemish nationalism. After the war they had to pay the wages of sin for that with a five year jail term and self-exile afterwards, mostly to Argentina.

My Great Aunt's husband Maurice was with the "White Brigade", a secret silent man who deigned to talk to me. I still wonder whether he wanted me to join, at but I went back to Ostend and found other means to work instead.

The coast was on full alert and put on the defensive now after they lost the Battle of Britain, having tried their reign of terror there too, they started losing so many planes there, they never achieved the superiority to make a landing remotely possible considering those barges.

All experiments taken in their proper perspective proved to be a lot of sand in the eyes to avert real attention from their plans, some of which were taken seriously enough.

For instance there were the concrete coffer dams or mulberries started on the small beach, they broke, being too weak and thinly built against the short snappy waves, some barges towed by tugs snapped their cables and became loose, speedboats with rudder sticks from which the outboards could be lifted above the water-level and made to skid over the minefields.

All that could have had a chance with the Merchant Navy helping and with the presence of a decent sized Navy fleet augmented with the submarines holding the pass wide open with a protective coverage of air power fully employed.

They attempted a small trial raid from France, we all heard about it, the Hitler Youth who were fully involved got burned and extensively hospitalized in St. Omairs afterwards.

The three walls of fire in the possible landings on the English coast where not fully envisaged and anticipated indeed: but secretly unknown they got a partial inkling at the time, considering all things were possible but maybe not advisable, they intended to drive the attention off this and direct it instead eastwards destroying at once the myth and unholy alliance with Stalin, the main "Blitz" Barbarossa, the invasion of Russia.

Little did they know that their quick temper would cloud their judgment and distract the leader of the "Luftwaffe", namely Goering from the destruction of the air fields in Britain, to the civilian population, losing the initiative already hanging on a thin thread by the anger aroused from the bombing of Berlin, and to turn the moment of time and history for which we could thank Churchill's decision to our advantage.
The sacrifice was enormous but it paid off. One thing would cause the other now and lead to a succession of the definite fall of the third Reich accordingly. The "Drang nach Osten" wasn't quick enough to encompass the whole of Russia in another big "Blitz"; which was stuck in the mud and some winter conditions very similar to Napoleons. Germany had run to far from her vital central lifelines and everything just became a prolongation of the dying dragon's death throes wagging its tail till the last enforced undulations would stop. The Gestapo was creeping like this all over the countries to catch in their dragnets the unfortunate, it was better to keep away from all controls under the puppet administrations, strangling and controlling our tentacles of governmental branches.

Youngsters could do this better assisted by their parents, my Mother sacrificed a lot in rations giving up her share to us and the fact that one could stay away out of circulation altogether and still get his share. At the end my Dad had to take anything going to stay around and look employed without being too obvious.

Sometimes we stayed with my Aunt Ray and she managed to get things from the Railway Guards but eventually we had to do without extra helpings of food supplies, we even went to funerals in the countryside just to eat and bring back something, you could get a pass for family business and we had a good fill up on such occasions but now we were unable to stock up and take things with us anymore.

Somehow the enemy gave you no choice even to breath after a time. This was well figured out, organized in detail and the blockade in itself helped awfully with the already overpopulation, it became increasingly more awkward. All things helped to get a good meal out of the bag. People living outside the twenty mile coastal zone had more access to the countryside and mobility than we had.

1941 passed into 1942, it was about time to make a go of it out of the encirclement. The best way was a well prepared overland crossing via the three "S's" Spain, Switzerland and Sweden. The more contacts we could gather the better, that was my ultimate aim.

It seemed to me there wasn't much time for romances and idylls, it had to wait till the war was over, and the eternal moving didn't help. All the girls we grew up with were biding their time waiting for the most eligible of the young men to return. Security was a big thing for them.

Most love affairs had to evolve by impulse and need, nature's ways. The meeting places like dance halls were closed by the occupation powers, but we held clandestine drinking parties with an advanced warning system operated to warn us of the patrols, then there was the eternal curfews to deal with.

The constant bombing and increasing flights over us to destroy Germany at night kept us fully awake by the flak alone, we slept as much in shelters as at home, also the Royal Navy had a go at the submarine and speedboat base which soon was completely blocked, because of this the submarines went more from their northern bases and St. Nazire straight for the open Atlantic: the speedboats quickly monitored, as soon as they dared to leave their moorings got strafed.

My brother Gerrard was born in all this turmoil and was called a typical war child. We were moved again out of our house to accommodate Luftwaffe personnel. Mostly it was for the Generals and officers which enabled them to hold their Roman orgies in the best houses available. Later those ladies of ill repute would run away with the best furniture, if they had not been already caught for doubtful practices, collaboration with intended theft.

Physically I kept up with my training and morally more determined than ever that I had to make it to England for the best of reasons.

The secret radio broadcasts kept encouraging us to go, come what may, instead of being sent to Germany. That was another restriction, not being allowed to tune in to the BBC. To be caught meant certain deportation to the camps as an enemy of the state.

One of my biggest disappointments was when a family quarrel broke out, let's say between husband and wife and she gave her husband away in spite which could cause the man to lose his life through it. Vice Versa too and so many other pitiful cases one heard about.

The German position in Russia was deteriorating. Setbacks were the order of the day. They weren't prepared to become stuck in the mud or ice. The North African campaign only bided some time.

The new weapons and the big guns near the channel came in the place of shortcomings in general. It was only a question of time which was not on their side, so we had to make the best of it, now.

With war on all fronts in full swing the communists brought in their groups of resistance too, which was an asset. This uneasy alliance was competitive but nevertheless an additional force.

Little groups came together to achieve breakthrough in aims to harass the enemy as much as possible and results increased with leaps and bounds. We stripped what we could before the enemy could get near. Once we were nearly caught as we contoured the Atlantic wall right behind the back of the Guard and then got chased up to the roof by another couple of soldiers who had watched us from a hidden place across the road. We hid in a vent, dug near the roof but eventually were flushed out at the end of the line. To our great surprise the soldiers let us go.

That was the only long view we had had since the beginning of hostilities of our beloved seaside.

Jewish people were beginning to get the brunt of their revenge, the rational for such behavior was explained in "Mein Kamph". For us it was rather a strange experience, Jewish children had been to school with us, amongst us, and nobody had ever thought anything about it, they had been blending in with us for centuries. They kept their own traditions which they had preserved and practiced at home to keep up the Jewish faith.

They had a synagogue behind one of our central churches and seemed to enjoy all the freedom of worship. We didn't really understand the sudden big fuss that was made about it at that time. The first thing to happen was that they all had to wear the yellow star with "Joude" on it, then they were gradually transported, they just disappeared! Some went into hiding, fearing the worst. Those were the wise ones of course.

6- Life in Occupied France:

By the time of the spring of 1942, which would have been my early call-up for the class of 1943, I was looking and trying to gather information on how to get closer to the Spanish border without being noticed.

Boosts to our moral were given by the knowledge that agents were being dropped everywhere with the equipment and monies to continue the struggle on a more even basis. Some were landed by short takeoff planes on the new autostrade strip at Jabeke near to Bruges.

Somewhere on the other side a party of blackshirts was taking place in an old castle and an aerodrome with the consequence that it got bombed out. That was the boost to our moral we had been looking for. Everything was working in good order now.

I met a third year electrician in the trade school called Everaert, an extremely selfish character he turned out to be but reliable, who's uncle was an opportunist of considerable dimensions turned collaborator. The uncle advertised the fact that he needed able bodied students for the vacation periods and others for the Normandy coast with good pay and food; that was it! John his name was, handled it as a subcontracting firm for the "Organisation Todt" for helping at construction, of which we had no knowledge. Curiosity got the better of us and were told, find out. We were all fully aware of the secret operations carefully implemented by our teachers documents were supplied by John.

The trip would go through Brussels, Paris, and Le Mans to Cherbourg and surrounding places. Contacts could be looked out for by us all along the route.

Everything was wished for and set for those assaults. I had probed the Dunkirk area first but that was hopeless too well-guarded, some of us got into the Calais region. I went there with an old friend George a boyhood acquaintance who had gained a lot of experience on the island of Jersey recently, from which he had escaped by hiding away on a provisions ferry.

We nearly got ourselves arrested in the same sand dunes of before by a German platoon on exercise, who took us for spies.

After this I lost track of George as he belonged to a new resistance group and found Daniel instead who was interested in getting to England. With John, and Everaert plus another eleven of us I had to find out for this mission if I could get through now one way or the other.

Our team consisted mostly of Ostend lads, quite a few had a British background like the Hendersons, Jarvises, and Maynards of families like mine from past campaigns and fully integrated.

Ostend had had still quite a decent sized Anglican community. We all had one single thing in mind, reaching England and hitting the enemy back as hard as we could from there.

Our John had his quota now and we set off on the day of the trial run fully operational. He had to watch the lot of us as he was solely responsible for us.

I suspected he realized what we had in mind, so much his nephew would have told him too, but his ideas where to make the knife cut both ways, for so much I realized from my own personal observations, and we were in relatively safe hands for this double game, for the moment.

The loyal bunch I should call the group now was off. The trip went according to plan, smoothly rolling along crossing the frontiers with flying colors, this time check points and free passage provided for, nine hours it took to reach Paris. Travelling in the silvery moonlight I thought, standing looking out in the corridor, we are making better headway than in that early May day of 1940 and in a much shorter time; we passed Compiegne, the Armistice place Hitler had stood on so much,

I was reflecting, my Grandmother had left for the old Inn on Slijkens, or muddy sluices, as we called it and wouldn't budge anymore for the rest of the war, which was for sure. Once the old lady made up her mind like a "Dulle Griet" an angry old lady, this character was known in Flemish folklore, illustrated by H. Bosh, it was also a big gun used in sieges, meaning in dialect somebody usually female who gets in a Fierce fighting mood.

My Aunt Ray had everything planned to get as quickly as possible back to my North Africa with her loot when it was all over; and to marry cousin Irene off to the Godfather of them all, contracted her to, and in return would have a hotel in Tangier that would suit her books perfectly.

Inflicting as much embarrassment on my Uncle as she could in the process, buying fur coats in his name, a leopard never changes it's spots, as the saying goes; I still maintain they loved each other for ever, it was Delilah, Cleopatra and Rachel all in one for her. Maybe there was a passionate delight in all this, I don't know! Greed and all other passions included. She could be caring to the destitute and fallen angels.

Stopping over at Paris to change stations we had enough time to kill for a visit to the local sights, we saw the Place de la Concorde, la Madeleine, King Albert's statue near the Seine, little and the Grand Palace, strolled along the Champs Elyse's to l'Arc de Triumph on l' Etoile where we walked and tramped on the old German-Austrian Empire eagles together with the French in solemn procession right in front of the noses of the German soldiers, enjoying a satisfying delight in all this; things started brightening up for us, the feeling of being trodden on was waning. We had a cup of ersatz coffee on the terrace with the music playing and managed to get to Monmartre and l'Opera; we ignored Cafe de la Faix as a lot of German officers and Nazi Officials were also there.

The coffee was ersatz and the sweetener saccharine there was not much else to get. We also went to a bistro near Montmartre and got more satisfaction with aperitifs. So all in all we had a good time for the war and Uncle John was pretty glad for his bunch, giving him no trouble so far. I noticed now his skull and crossbones silver ring, he was showing off and displaying the ugly thing. How deep was he involved? And was he proud enough to be or was he playing the bluffing part?

We were soon cozily tucked away on our train to the South-West and for Le Mans now, the landscape changing to sunnier and more pleasant countryside, not so harsh looking as the North was.
As we listened to the French around us talking we gathered that they had more than enough of the Boche by now. Eventually pointing to us we were taken to be a northern Boche too with a more proud bearing.

We had another stopover at Lemans for Cherbourg, long enough for another visit to town. This was the cross roads, we indulged in a good hearty meal in the German army canteen placed in the station for which John had coupons at the ready. The meal was typical Nordic, a thick soup and a big plate of meat, potatoes and vegies, with custard pie for dessert.

The thought that the Germans were bastards but their soup was good was communicated with our eyes going around the table to see if John reacted but he was unperturbed and played it cool. The other Germans thought we were speaking one of their northern dialects. To them it sounded something like English and vice versa to the English and French maybe even Yiddish to the unskilled ear. We couldn't win that way for sure.

We all started enjoying the trip. John pretty sure of himself told us that we could visit the town. Eagerly accepting the situation we took off in groups. We walked up the sloping avenue till we reached what looked like the central square and it is always amazing how one can always pick up exactly what one is looking for, in this case, a biggish bistro with the girls which turned out to be a brothel of course.

After ordering the wine and the girls coming to join us we had one called Suzanne Bardot, to this day I still wonder about the connection.

There were also Germans around going up and down the stairs in full force. At the same time you could notice the French patriots everywhere talking and sitting conveniently at the tables.

Somehow they seemed to understand that we didn't come for the usual only information and nothing else. That is the way it was done and we had fallen straight into it: so she told us very trustingly that every week or so an English agent came for pick-ups and took them to the coast of the Vendee or Bretagne, to be transferred from the French fishing boats to a Royal Navy trawler somehow under the nose of the Germans and further out.

There it was, the contact, just like that, on this she left us and attended to the other customers instead.

Exactly what we looked for we had gathered, now to stay behind, loose John and make good for a week or so as we had no rations or passes and didn't know anybody around, not much money left on us either. It had to be done alone, a group of three or four was to compromising. So we left the Bistro deep in our thoughts seriously pondering the whole subject. I decided I would make a go of it, somehow, strolling back to the station because time was up.

John was ready for us and at any moment our train could arrive. Once on it, it would take me to far away. I had to look for an opportunity to stay in the station. The locomotive came hissing and steaming in on the other track like a huge monster.

My nerves were tense and I kept to the rear of the group quickly looking everywhere. John in the lead ran with the pack to the tunnel for the other track, I was on their backs reluctantly following and trying to lag behind them when they all entered in the tunnel. I passed stealthily along the other side of the wall and stairways instead. Down they all went in a rush not observing my absence in their hurry and excitement going up on the other side and climbing on the train which suddenly departed quickly in the same manner as it had arrived, nobody missed me and I kept a bit in the shadows out of their view. Good bye!

When the train was a good distance I had to laugh loosening the tension of my subdued fears and now in relief, I had made it for the first stage.

I could just imagine John looking all over the train compartments and starting to ask questions. I hoped they would keep quiet for my sake.

The first thing was getting my bearings here. I started chatting to two French porters telling them I was lost after missing my train which was the unvarnished truth after all.

They told me the best thing to do was to go to the Renault works as they needed people and from there get myself established. Well and good I walked towards the place after looking around to find it and got myself an enormous apetit in the process; it was the weekend and everything was closed. On going back to get my few belongings I took a chance in the German canteen again.

Indeed I got myself another hearty meal but also the attention of a nosy lieutenant asking me all kinds of questions, he tried German in my dialect but ended up talking English which we both had a working knowledge of. From there he somehow got to a telephone after excusing himself and soon I was picked up by the German police and taken to their headquarters.

I don't know whether John had signaled from somewhere and somehow, but they treated me well on someone's orders, they were not yet Gestapo, and I had a comfortable room delegated but was closely watched. Next day John arrived and gave me a good telling off, I told him like all the others that I had missed the train by accident, he said that is alright for them but not for him as my mates had told him all.

He would save me for the return favor he hoped for, and to keep quiet for the rest.

We quickly returned and he was glad to have his man back after all, he was responsible for me and couldn't afford any feelings either: put it all down to inexperience he said. The same evening we were back in the fold with the others after a hectic travel across Normandy and arrived with the group next morning by bus in what they called "Le Petite Swiss Normande" after traversing a long high wooded hill, the tallest I guessed to be on my right, at the other side we were billeted in prepared barracks near a little place called "Plessis Grimoult", very nice countryside, plenty of food was available, fresh eggs had already become a luxury for us and the famous Camembert cheese of course, cider and calvados. We still had to try all this as soon as possible and eat to our hearts desire. The Tod organisation was present with architects and supervisors, also with a few ramrods assisting.

It was a quasi-militarized organization of drop-outs: any rejects and a few old ones. They were dressed in light khaki uniforms.

In the morning we were briefed after John had introduced us and departed to go back somewhere, Belgium I presume.

We were taken in their own buses to the job, up to the highest point of the hill I had seen the evening before, to an open clearing in the woods at the summit. I found from what I could make out a pyramid built tower structure with a center control and a bit further along a huge screen similar to the screen of a drive in cinema but grilled and facing the seaside.

Little did we know what all the secrecy was about, apparently it was Radar, reasoning something out of this contraption and its station. Possibly it was not as sophisticated as the British system which had stopped them winning the Battle of Britain but they were catching up quickly. Their specialists resembled air force personnel as they moved about in the main building doing inspections. More contracted labor was hired to join us. French from around and a couple from East

Flanders imported like us; real laborers, we never could catch up with them. They were certainly more cut out for this kind of hard work and used to it. Needless to say, we weren't used to this type of activity at all. We had never lifted as much as a shovel load or raised a pick, Everaert, John's nephew, was given preference and had a chance to use his electrical knowledge he had just acquired at school to practice with.

There were adders in this place and we saw quite a lot of them, also beautiful multicolored grass snakes, the heat of the sun brought them out in mass onto the hillside which we had been digging and which in consequence had disturbed them. The country girls were attractive and in full bloom of youthfulness. Camouflage nets were placed to cover the works. Needless to say, the British came and had a good look at this glorified construction, to see what it was all about.

As far as it being a holiday camp it was jolly hard work, the rock face was hard and difficult, we never could beat the East Flanders men who were the old ones, which made them laugh when shoveling the rocks used to fill the small tipping railway wagons or dollies, as they were called.

Our ridiculous efforts made us angrier; on the other hand we didn't want to work too hard for the enemy at all, the slower the works the lesser use of radar but the ramrods and supervisors saw to it that we kept hard at work. Moving the tip loaders track I found back breaking, I seemed to get all the load to myself.

One day they made a mistake when concreting one of the outside pyramid towers, another person and myself where put to chip it off with a hammer and chisel which looked more like a punishment to me. They gave nothing to protect the eyes, such as goggles, so that the specially prepared brittle concrete with small pebbles mixed into it flew into our eyes which became all red and cut after a time. We needed to keep washing them out and they became infected. We thought the Hebrew slaves must have felt as we now did when they were building the pyramids.

The air was fresh and unspoiled except for the dust produced by our labors. They had the edge on us, anyway. Their wages were better, too, so we had to continue.

When we had finished the building and screen on this hill they then started to take us further afield to Beaumont on the left side cape of Cherbourg Peninsular, then to St. Pierre l'Eglise which was in front of a large convent but not to be confused with St. Mere l'Eglise close to Utah Beach which was in the American Sector.

After the move to St. Pierre l'Eglise itself which was later used during the invasion, I believe for the U.S.A. landing site near to Utah Beach. Beaumont had another radar screen which was very vulnerable to frequent strafing and attack.

St. Pierre had sheltered headquarters control in front of the convent and between the seafronts for control of the gun placements.

Some of the Tod's men where the principal characters and I later found out some of the guards over the prisoners were also.

To begin with this one in particular was the typical sergeant a disciplinarian plus ruffian, ordering everybody around in the worst possible manner of a bully. We thought he was in need of a couple of hard lessons in the future.

First of all he had a pair of tropical short trousers on, made of some peculiar material by one of us from Bruges, a self-styled tailor, to get himself out of the bulk of the hard work.

When it was finished with it was too tight so when "discipline" bent on the job to give an example to us they split from one end to the other to our delight, of course never mind his surprised looks and anger, the worst of it was that he could have sworn at the tailor who was absent and had been pre warned by us to make himself scarce: when the sergeant found this out he nearly exploded on the spot. Before we knew it the tailor was back on the job with us, for a while.

The next incident followed quickly after this one, he collected all the cement bags scattered on the ground and picking on us as an example called us dirty French, he then made a huge pile and set light to it. The flames went up very high and burned the camouflage nets which had caught the heat from the conflagration the flames licking greedily at each other. His smile quickly froze when he saw the chain reaction he had started: most of us acted as though we hadn't seen anything till he started screaming fire and then he started to panic, running frantically carrying buckets of water until it was under control, he then suddenly disappeared from the scene in shame and we were never bothered again.

One day the sergeants enormous strength saved the lives of two Frenchmen, who would have been crushed by a small engine tilting sideways onto them, while he hung on to the engine and prevented its fall until more help arrived. After this incident human relations were much improved and our tailor got his job back and was allowed to do things for us.

Off duty sometimes troubles were brewing unexpectedly, usually in the bistro where the hotheads of both sides would gather after drinking the strong wine and cider often getting into patriotic arguments.

We had a fearless strong man named Jan and it didn't take long after the German soldiers started singing "We are sailing against England" and referring to the bombing of Coventry that a fight started in earnest amongst us and Jan got stabbed in the back by a short dagger like bayonet as he was tackling two of them at the same time. The rest got rounded up by the military police and transferred to "Tod's" security jail. Jan, who was taken to hospital, lost a lot of blood but survived, he was given sick leave and never came back.

The rest of us had a day in the cooler and afterwards we had to run behind their bicycles towards the convent which was a couple of miles away before we were dismissed.

My friend Pierre from the former row-boat incident joined us to and another one of his exploits was to swim and make a dive in the old French laundry stand, situated on squares and corners along a small rivulet. Of course he never considered or tested the depth and got his stomach scratched open from the bottom of it, another casualty we could have done without.

Pierre was healed within a week and by then the guard becoming slack, we were able to cut our way out through the fence with the aid of a big cutting wrench, taken from the stores, and made for the beach everything going our way, crossing the abandoned cider apple orchards we tried the best of the fruit for eating, otherwise the apples were much to sharp and then we took a long desired swim on that beach which we enjoyed but found it colder than to the north of us: the rocky ground and quick depth caused the coolness which we found at first to be exhilarating but not too comfortable for a long swim either.

It was just as well because as we were busy drying ourselves and almost ready to go back suddenly all hell broke loose around us, in the distance and out to sea. Guns went off all at once and the pace was kept up constantly and we saw some specks like small blobs moving far out to sea like seals. We figured out later and after the war that it had been the two men submarines attempting to get samples from the beach rocks for future landings.

Before our last stay everybody was getting on the nerves of the other, falling through each other's wooden bunks daily, mostly the result of practical jokes with Pierre getting the brunt of it, we all had had enough of it by now. This reminded me of an incident when I was up in my favorite tree, which I could climb in a jiffy then, Pierre with enormous difficulty struggled up while I waited in the foliage for him to appear, eventually he made it and myself fed up by now went quickly down in reverse, nonchalantly sitting a bit further away to get a breather looked back and there were two policemen standing under the tree calling him down and reprimanding his behavior. I couldn't help laughing when he approached with a long face and mold me off for not having warned him. I hadn't seen them and didn't know they were near us, just one of those things that sometime happen to us all.

I guess he never believed it but always got more and more setbacks although he was considered a genius that was his way, to bumble through things.

We had a holiday and on the last day we had a shopping spree in Cherbourg. As there was no suitable transport available we took our chances and travelled partly in a French dustcart standing upright in one of the empty bins holding our noses and then in a picturesque little tram, rolling along the coast which was an excellent way of sightseeing, puffing along the sheer cliffs with sea and rocks alternatively coming into view.

We reached Cherourg in safety and learned that a raid had been made on the beach incurring a number of casualties who had been mistaken for Germans. This was our lot for being caught between the various fighting factions. An unpleasant necessity inflicted upon us by their presence everywhere we were also taken advantage of by the circumstances of the type of war that we were involved in.

Otherwise we had a pleasant day in that town gathering presents and tins of biscuits unattainable at home. Our exploits and earnings here enabled the people at home to have an extra ration for once in a while we were being fed here, one of the other objects we bought was a beautiful knife with an inlaid bone handle, a Spanish style flick knife, made for hand to hand fighting, which we knew we could use to defend ourselves if necessary.

Like this we departed, with Pierre never to come back, and myself I missed him or another couple of months, which I spent in another place south of Cherbourg named Brickebec and Quetehou.

7- Joining the Resistance:

Whilst I was there I became ill and during my stay in the barracks with a fever I became acquainted with a secret group of Gaullists and other resistance groups doing the same as us, infiltrating and monitoring.

They talked me into being available for operations at any time for their cause. Things were going our way. The only one left with me was Everaert now who joined them and was there when the invasion took place. I didn't recuperate well enough and was sent home on sick leave.

We had a last training session in the wooded areas at the back of the barracks reminiscent of the trenches in the last war. I nearly lost an eye in the mock battle and received a permanent mark on my pupil. I think that completed my training and now I had many sources of contact.

My trip back comprised and included Brussels and this time I stayed longer with my Mother's family her eldest brother who had his own business: his wife Helen a Greek woman knew a lot of people in the neighborhood, she was also caretaker of the Greek Orthodox church and looked after the community there. My cousin Henri went to the University of Louvain and took part in resistance pranks which was very strong among the students, from taking down flags to being couriers for the secret services and organized underground groups. As they knew of my endeavors to find proper contacts, they quietly circulated the news. I still had to physically improve and my weakened condition left me feeling short of breath and coughing, I also had my arm lanced because of infected boils; my Mother was worried so I took it easy for the winter and continued studying at the trade school, it was a welcome interval, we all came to know each other again. There was no respite from the regular bombing which was intended for the convoys and flak-guns. Our Allies considered our position and tried for the military targets only.

I gave information on all the things and installations I had seen to the monitoring teachers at school and this information found its way to England and everything was kept up to date.

Some cinemas had reopened and were showing German U.F.A. films and propaganda pieces grossly overrated. Austrian films showing comics were not too bad. In this way we heard of Zarah Leander who turned out to be a Russian spy in the midst of the German High Command. We also saw Marika Rok a Hungarian dancer and cabaret star.

There was also boxing still at its peak with Karel Sys going to fight Ole, Tandberg in Sweden. He was a Cassius Clay style of boxer and not damaged in any way, in fact the whole team were excellent boxers. They would pay for their collaboration after the war with their promoter Theo Vanhaverbeke.

I didn't hear about John anymore. I couldn't trust him too much and one day I was watched by a black shirt whilst at the Doctors. I was sure it was me he was after, one get that certain feeling of being under observation. There is little I can say about this episode except that I passed the time studying more, and one evening under the curfew, on a very dark night, falling into the cellar of a bombed house after leaving the cinema. I lost consciousness for a moment and then somebody helped me out of the hole. I had cut the side of my face open which held me up again for a time. In the interim I met two old friends, George and Daniel, again and I asked them whether they would come and join me in going to England or North Africa.

They became interested and by the spring of 1942 we were ready for this operation to begin.

I took George first on a trial run and Daniel was unable to be found. I must say George was an expert at forging passes and official stamps so we were provided for with them, as we passed the coastal limit zone across Pachendale's old bridge controlled by the Germans who saluted us, the passes were so perfect.

Once outside the zone we changed our direction and made for the French Border which we passed somewhere between Mouscron and Halloyn without any trouble. Arriving in Lille where we made a short visit we slept in the roomy hall of the station and gathered as much information from travelers as we could.

There was work in Albert near Arras so we headed for there on the direct line. On the train we got even better news about the ancient Soissons and Reims regions, they were building certain fortifications on the old ridge over there, we had to find out more, this could be important, maybe a second line or for the use of special weaponry. It turned out to be both. The contractors where busy engaging people when we arrived so we fell straight in there, we were installed in an old glass factory Courcy-Aux-Loges near the crest of the hill. Firstly we looked after the storage of the incoming material near a bend of the river the Germans used for swimming, we had two guards with us all the time who looked like Austrians, more like Laurel and Hardy types.

One day we took off and hid in the straw to have a nap after investigating all the thick copper insulated wire coils we found stacked up, there was more of that than anything else to come. Something important was brewing in those hills.

We thought the guards would soon go but they stayed there longer than we expected, all this time guarding a big barreled fire extinguisher on wheels in between them, we kept looking behind the bale to see them go but they didn't, after a time annoyed and fed-up the Laurel one kicked the barrel in some place and found by accident a valve that opened and spluttered completely over them, in a short time they were covered in a white liquid.

The Hardy one swearing and telling off the other one, we burst out laughing in the back and crept stealthily out, as they left after us, we had no time to set the place alight because of the soldiers entertaining themselves in front. They took us for the helpers delegated to the two half blind and gesticulating pair who didn't take the slightest notice of us at all.

In one of those light moments we just managed to get out in time but kept in mind a chance for a later attempt, maybe night time would be better.

Soissons was a nice little town full of young girls of our age looking for entertainment and pleasure as the war was dragging along, not marriage either, more serious matters could wait. This kept us fairly busy the town's attractions of cinemas, dance halls and general sightseeing and roaming the wild hills nearby.

Soisson is known for the vase of the same name where Clovis the King of the Franks is supposed to have meted out a Solomon's judgment on two of his warriors arguing and drawing sword over the Roman Celtic booty. He just hacked the enormous and precious vase to pieces solving the problem at once, which is to this day depicted by the statue in the village square.

I believe Joanne D'Arc slept and passed through here too, anyway the food was still edible, good bread and madeleines for us to fill up on. The dance halls were swinging to the sound of Tartacala the gypsy girl.

The sun shone in the morning on our trenches as we dug the windswept ridges to drop the big cables in and ourselves after the roasting of potatoes enriched with butter or fat, cooked on a stick over open fires.

Occasionally we dug up the bones of old fallen soldiers from the 1914-1918 War, which were ceremonially reburied by the villagers, in the war graves cemetery. Things went along like this for some time until one day I couldn't find George returning late from one of his escapades with the girls.

He left a note for me which said the Gestapo was after him, he'd packed up and returned to Ostend. I thought I had better follow without making myself too conspicuous, I took a last walk around the countryside aware that something was going on, there was more than the eye could meet. Nearing the top of the slope I turned to the right and noticed split sticks with a piece of paper containing words at intervals with more of the same containing messages that could be rearranged pertaining to assembly points and times of droppings. I walked on until I came to an open field, more like a short landing strip to me, which indeed it was. After this I came back to the starting point and noticed a little hamlet almost hidden by the foliage which stirred my curiosity. I first went to the Cafe-Bistro where some of the locals were playing billiards and they invited me to have a game, it is probable they had seen me and had watched my movements for a while before this, after a few periods we chatted away and it turned out that they took me into their confidence. They were doing resistance work and interested in getting new recruits. After taking my leave I was glad of the information I had gathered and quickly left Courcy-aux-Loges bearing in mind that the trail was hot because of my friend George. I returned to Compiegne junction to get the first train back to Brussels. I was lucky because my pass was in good order still and I found no harassment on the train.

I went straight to my Aunt Helen and after a good reception and telling them about the urgency to get to England because of the close association I had had with George and his pursuers. My Aunt got a neighbor to come over who cross-examined me and asked about all the information I had gathered in Soissons concerning the cables and bunkers in the ridge which was intended for some of the new weapons they had in mind and the General Headquarters which were to be installed there in case of invasion.

The lady in question was told by Aunt **of** my wish to get to England and the fact that I was being pursued because of my previous exploits. She looked at me straight in the eye and said:

"You go to St. Jean-De Luz, to Hotel-Du-Tourism and tell them you are sent by me, mentioning her name "Madame De Nile", and that was it; from all the contacts I had that one was the most important and I just knew I had to take her advice. With this information I proceeded on my way to Ostend, looked up George but he had literally gone underground and instead I met Daniel who had just received his shoes, ready to be transported to Germany, as he was there and available with his papers "There is no time to lose" I said you' come with me.

It was the Goodbye's to my Mother that I will remember forever: she knew that something was in the offing and came with me to the small cross-country train which I was taking as a precaution. The departure was very moving of course like the soldiers going to the front in "Farewell to Arms".

Comfortably seated we made for the frontier after leaving with her the messages for possible rendezvous points, verbally, for George if he followed on later.

At the border we waited till the guard was changed and the French Guards came along and when we were alone we had cigars to give to them, the growing of tobacco in Belgium had no restrictions unlike in France. It was taken as a gift, they knew that we were all involved by now and so were they but we helped each other.

In no time we made for Compiegne and I didn't like the Police there who were watching the station, they gave us a long look, carefully I went to Courcy dodging them and fulfilling my mission and using the pass without arousing any suspicion. Once there it didn't take me long to find out the place was to hot and reeking of treason.

We quickly retraced our steps and took a different route making for Paris instead. George couldn't have possibly found us if he escaped from any incarceration, but you never know, I also knew that he would still try.

The advantage with Daniel, was that he had an uncle seventy kilometers south of Paris in Pithiviers district well hidden behind the Orleans Forest, he was a horse dealer and well known to the other farmers. This was the place to hide for a while with lots of food available and dense woods to hide in.

We just skimmed Paris and got out as quickly as we could in a great haste. We made good time to Pithiviers and everything was as expected and we received a marvelous welcome. Daniels Uncle collected us at the station as he was pre- warned by telephone and his Aunt and Uncle talked for hours afterwards. Daniel's cousins were a nice couple of boys working hard and helping out on the farm most of the time. Their Dad said when the time came he would hide them in the nearby forest where there was already a group of the resistance and they would join them.

There were still wild boars in those woods. We saw the damage they did on his land to his vegetables the following morning. We stayed over a week and left loaded with an extra bags just filled to the brim with food. On the way we stopped in a town with a big cathedral along the railway; I think it must have been a famous one. Apart from that we arrived in Bordeaux safely, in a lonely bistro close to the harbor.

After a good meal without ration cards we got to talking with what turned out to be people who knew and pointed out a contractor who was looking for workers to help him in the "Landee" repairing a bridge. The Company was from Paris called "Sotramet" and the ideal chance for us to proceed with caution to our destiny.

George we never saw again till after the war, he told us that he went as far as Bordeaux and then turned back.

The Contractor took us to a place called Belin-Belier. A Gestapo man in plain clothes looked at our papers but the boss said we were in his employ and he would look after us so we were left pretty well alone.

This break was needed to enable us to slowly explore the re-entry of the coastal zone and also to build up our finances again so that we would have money when we needed to move on.

The work was pretty hard, it consisted of repairing a worn out and frail bridge. There were a lot of mosquitos in this place, it being moors and fen country, forested and with lots of beautiful grass snakes and turtles. The food was different here and the work harder than we envisaged.

Artichokes and beans every day with little or no meat. Ration cards were arranged and issued to us so this made us in order for the rest of the area.

The crew like us consisted mostly of hide-aways, some from as far as Paris, some were Spanish republicans and maquisards at the ready, and it was like a transit camp. We had our problems with the swift current underneath, boards dropping down and then hawking to get them back. Once we had an argument with a bad tempered Spaniard who disappeared at different times in a deep hole of the river while pulling the planks back and dragging a pontoon, but it turned out alright in the end. The friendship was tense but bearable. We had started to sing the Volga boat song, for him, and he was not amused about that.

We even managed to see a bull-fight in Bordeaux at the weekend put on by Portuguese, but shame on them, the Spaniards had to save the situation and jumped into the ring to finish the job, just when the air alarm went off. When everything was over we all left and had a swim instead.

My dive from the high board was quite enough and turned into a complete flop so I had had enough of it.

Returning home we were harassed by the same Gestapo man of before and again the Manager always present and on the same train could vouch for us and get us out.

That is something, I remarked to Daniel, we have got to avoid travelling on this line.

One day Daniel got so fed up, he wanted to get some more food from his Uncle and took off. After three days he came back with a hoard, I thought I had lost him too, but now I said we must take our leave and with our new provisions we easily made it across the fields.

He had met the same Nazi again with others who seemed to be very busy with their investigations.

Rommel's North African Corps had retreated from Benghazi and Tobruk and were sent to rest still wearing their tropical uniforms. In the evenings we found them everywhere singing and drinking the local mostly white wine.

I think we had to go anyway; I put it to the manager and, he was sorry to see us go and offered to help us with saying he'll move us to the Maquis of the Coreze if we wanted to. The border was very dangerous with all those troops there and the Gestapo in full force. Our mind was made up and the worst gaps on the bridge had been finished.

After the pay-out next day we went to rest as well; after a good meal in the old cemetery, the only peaceful place was among the graves and for not being watched or bothered, the grass was green too.

The Germans were busy, we watched them doing a lot of exercising keeping their troops on the go, we observed their assault tactics and were quite impressed, falling down on their knees after creeping and running on the imaginary enemy and rolling away from the shooting, it was excellent training.

We fell asleep and a nightmare suddenly woke me up and I felt an enormous fear, I am sure it was a premonition or warning of disaster and I should have taken heed.

Presenting itself in black and silvery flames a very pale old man of death had visited me in the dream and as a warning of imminent danger. Trying to shake the unpleasant feeling off and not taking any notice because I thought it was a reflection of the presence of the gravestones before falling asleep plus the fact that the steak we had eaten was a bit rotten; I boiled it down to this combination and packed our belongings to take the first bus to a place called Mont-de-Marsan which we reached in the evening in a bus full of schoolchildren all happy and gesticulating.

The country was rising now and we could see the foothills of the Pyrennes in the haze.

We left the country of D' Artagnan behind called Aquitaine and moved towards the country of the Basques now from lots of sheep rearing and horses to lovely mountain views, outcrops and rocks and some bull-rings where they fought the bulls with balls on their horns. There they performed it in the French way.

The old game of bull jumping between the horns from Mycenea and a gesture of bravery with the old Roman circuses incorporated in their displays.

Looking for the usual hidden restaurant and Hotel which didn't take too long and ideally situated near a mountain stream we checked in. Casually asking for a room they gave me the usual routine answer, "Go and ask the permission from the Kreiscomrnandatura".

Once they found out that we were trustworthy they let us in, they knew the name of the game, so did we. It was a dangerous game like everything else, it could cost them dear if they were ever found out, from a severe fine to closure or even deported and who knows what from there to the camps.

Anyway there was still a good bit of honor around and nobody gave anybody away unless one paid in another way for the vilest treason.

We had a little walk out first but came quickly back, the little town was teeming with troops and we told them permission had been granted, looking at us they said no need for that; Smiling and letting us in now. As it was, they gave us the room under the stairways and entrance. Well tucked away and with no windows for a quick escape, just a small partridge hole.

We asked the maid to tell us the time early in the morning when she brought the coffee and bread so that we could catch the early bus, there was only one per day and we had to make good on that one, we couldn't stay around any longer.

The idea was to get off at the coastal zone and begin walking from there and sell our luggage to make some extra cash. The rest was up to luck, intuition and skill in dodging the patrols from there.

In the morning we were taken completely by surprise as the maid was late, then Daniel had to play and flirt with her and I had the feeling the bus had gone at seven which it had and I was already becoming angrier by the minute. When we arrived at the bus stop we were told that it had left, indeed, and that was the end of my patience.

I said to Daniel that I had got the feeling it was no good to stay here another day so let's take the train and jump from it before it enters the station at Dax, maybe there was a stop before that. Everything was running out, time and patience as well, I started to feel very touchy with him. I couldn't drag my feet anymore so close to our target now, the other possibilities still could be used if this one failed; this was a mistake.

After quarreling back and forth we decided that it was now or never together. So far alright, the dice was thrown now. After all this game was nothing but a gamble. Approaching Dax rolling along at a steady pace everything looked so peaceful and quiet we took a chance to try the station carrying our luck to far.

8- Capture and Imprisonment:

We got off the train a short distance before the station but, there was no chance at all, we had had it, the place was suddenly swarming with troops, sergeants and officers in plain clothes looking like American tourists shouting and giving loud orders. This was a trap set by the Gestapo and we had fallen right into it. I told Daniel to get onto the next train just the same, suddenly the usual one we had seen several times before was in front of us on the platform taking snapshots or pictures of us.

The train started moving, nobody got out of the station and he went from compartment to compartment shouting "don't move" and taking our papers away. Soldiers were guarding the corridors all along the speeding train. Trapped like a bunch of herded animals I could have kicked myself. The Gestapo man rushed to the rear using the same tactics. I said to Daniel "Come with me" into the corridor, never mind the papers and luggage but he was so slow.

We chatted the young soldier up and he took us for one of them obviously, I checked the next door from my position to where Daniel still stood talking and made a sign to him to come over, I already had the handle in my hand but Daniel was to slow, just about to utter the word jump when all of a sudden the Gestapo came in, Luger in hand, pointed at us and telling the soldier off very harshly and shouting what in the hell did we think we were doing up there.

Too late now we had lost our chance, we got pushed into the compartment again and he brought with him a few minutes later another victim pushed around by his helpers. This woman turned out to be the real prey they were after, we were just extra fish caught in the dragnet. I wonder whether he recognized us from before.

There were about fifteen of us in the same group that were caught, that is a considerable haul I think. From then on he got very pompous and busy. Interrogating chiefly the woman and concentrating on her, she was still young but not a teenager either. I never got her name which wouldn't be real anyway, as she turned out to be an agent or spy according to our Gestapo man looking at us intently and then back to her, saying it is because of people like you that all of those boys are going to be shot, now. Well on this there was no doubt whatsoever about our fate. I had had enough of Daniel dragging his feet and it was everybody for himself now to make the best of it and to get away when the first opportunity arose.

The trip to Biarritz was very somber if not depressing; the sun was shining the shimmering haze clearing up over the countryside making it even brighter. No concerted attempt was made to escape by those individuals left to their own thoughts as he disappeared from our compartment to others. Obviously he had other victims there who were just as important.

It was a pity because it had to be done now, the most likely moment to escape while we were still very fit, jump the guards and gestapo and in the confusion roll off the train into the isolated countryside using the free ride to get closer to our destination.

The massacre would have been ugly but what were the odds, they had heard of it too besides their own knowledge of what awaited them, torture and afterwards execution. In this way we reached the Biarritz junction and I had just seen a glimmer of sunlight reflecting on what looked like a small yacht harbor or bay full of white painted boats whose brilliance caused me to shade my eyes.

I knew the Gestapo in the occupied zones were stretched to breaking point so I had to quickly look for my own opportunity. I had also heard of patriots being previously caught in the fields made to dig their own graves before being shot.

This made me even more determined. As the train came to a stop we were herded off and lined up in the hall under the scrutiny and watchful eyes of the guards, rifles at the ready. There were people behind them and I noticed an elderly lady wearing sunglasses that nodded as she made a recognition amongst us.

We were marched off now and I saw more of the bay to my right which I tried to memorize. I made up my mind that this would be the place to make my get-a-way diving into the water and swimming below the surface and hardly showing myself slowly advancing under to the other side of the boats, I had trained for that and liked it, I would have to get rid of my clothes under water as they would become heavy. If they were shooting the bullets would be ricocheting on the surface and they' would think after a while that I had drowned.

Afterwards I found out there was no water behind the quay at all just soft mud which I couldn't see from where I was walking, nothing but quagmire and very smelly mud with rocks here and there scattered around. That would have been the end of the road for me.

So in a little while we arrived at the Hotel, their center for all operations in the region. It was quite a famous hotel because of King Edward the Seventh holidaying there and that was its name. Now it was the Gestapo Headquarters.

I looked very intently around before entering to assess the situation with the corners next to the bay.

We were led to different rooms, our belongings taken away for inspection and they immediately started to interrogate us, there were quite a few waiting which seemed the usual routine here.

So many at this time were trying to get away or walking the plank I should say that it was a kind of mass production.

After everybody was questioned we had the privilege of being kept back, after the guard had found out and let us go here we were again, what excuses we had now.

So on his quick rattling of questions at us I told him we looked for work, as the other job was finished and here we had all that we needed.
As they went through our pockets and even afterwards checked our naked bodies, he found a photo of my grandparents, parents and I in front of the cafe in Ostend.

Nothing special about that except it showed Pale-Ale and Guinness-Stout advertised on the windows. One Gestapo shouted that's English and said "look at the types" and indeed we had a good family background back for three hundred years, but our first Gestapo knew better that and he answered to the other one, they have types among the Flemish like that also, they used to import those beers, which we did, actually it became another question which was also very innocent when they found a schedule for the trains to St. Jean De Luze, that was another place near the border every time and so was the destination of all the other suspects.

9- Brief Escape:

There his reasoning stopped abruptly and he had to keep his end up with the others now, even if we were suspects. I realized I had to leave now or never. There was nothing else left to do. I knew about their cruel torturing methods once in their hands and the weakening of the spirit and body with it, nobody knew, you had to make up your mind to resist beforehand. I didn't feel ready for all of that, yet.

Looking around like a cornered animal I noticed a Gestapo man tired and dozing in the next room which had access to a balcony where the double glass doors were open because of the midday heat. Daniel was just putting his clothes on and I was already dressed, the other prisoners were being shuffled away to the lower jails or cells.

This was my opportunity, I had a folded knife in my hand which had been overlooked during my search as it was held in my clenched fist when my hands were up and Daniel was nearly ready so I shouted, came quickly to him but he froze as usual, far to slow with his guard holding him. I was off like an arrow from a bow, swift, light footed with my sandals on for fast running. The dozing man never woke up as I passed him in my lightning run, which I had already anticipated, literally diving from the railings on the balcony disregarding the drop from the first floor to the pavement. I put my hands on the balustrade to make a good jump which I had rehearsed a thousand times before, unfortunately my foot must have dragged a bit because one of the straps on my sandal must have caught, so my foot touched the upper bar and I started falling turning in mid-air and coming with a thump down on the pavement landing on my behind and back the impact of which gave me a slight concussion but luckily for me no broken bones, just a dent in my pride for the poor jump. Within a few seconds I noticed the hulk of a grinning uniformed Gestapo man above me, leaning over the balcony and struggling to get his pistol out of the holster and putting his finger on the trigger, to his complete amazement and mine nothing happened, the bullet was a dud.

I quickly got up and made for the first corner I could see to try to avoid the shooting which I knew would follow, running in a zig-zag fashion to make it more difficult to take aim. So far so good, I escaped just the same, not the way I expected it, but away, just seconds before taking the blind corner for cover, the salvos went off and one of them pierced my right hand entering through my wrist and coming out of the palm of my hand slightly touching my fingers it felt like a heavy blow. The rest of the bullets flying around my ears which were deafening. I held my hand more by impulse than pain and turned the corner, blood was pouring which caused me to hurry more once through and free from the firing. The next three hundred meters I ran in record time and turning in from the furthest corner I noticed a small German van swerving wildly coming out from my right, hoping it was empty I turned swiftly around it then acting nonchalantly like a pedestrian passing by, tried to jump in the rear to escape my pursuers altogether. To my surprise it was packed full with German soldiers holding on to their rifles, maybe called out for my capture.

I knew I couldn't run to far now and turned into the street from which they had come. They were shouting and screaming to the driver behind me to stop. The street looked long and empty making a perfect target for a hunted animal, me in this case. That's the way I felt, my hand was still bleeding after rubbing it on my face to keep the hair out of my eyes. Otherwise I could have jumped the portals.

There was only thing left to do, jump over the first fence, which was a privet I saw on my right, which I did and ran to the rear of the building entering the kitchen of this corner house. Once in there to the complete surprise of both of us, there was a housewife pressing her clothes on the ironing board. One can imagine our expressions and only my presence of mind could save the situation now and speaking in French "Les Boches me cherchent je veus me cache" and her instant panic was enough to tell me that it wasn't going to work, dropping her iron and screaming. I was done for where I stood.

Coming out faster than I had gone in I trusted to my luck. I headed towards the wall of the next house climbing on a coal box and got over the wall in no time, leaning on my hand which was feeling very painful by now. I was in a small cul-de-sac and for me luckily again a back door was open which I quickly entered still hearing that silly woman screaming which gave my whereabouts away and impeded my escape.

I never understood her attitude unless she was struck by sudden shock and fear which she couldn't overcome, she was dumb and panic stricken. It proved to be part of the bad dream I had in Belin-Belier when I slept near the tomb stones, and still my struggling was far from over. One against too many this seemed to be the story of my destiny.

I was completely encircled and upwards was the only way left to me, as I climbed the stairs looking down from the first turn I could see their shadows from a covered position in the woman's garden.

I had no weapons except my knife to fight. My only chance was the roof. Somehow I couldn't reach the gutter without being an open target from the outside as I had to lean out and would become visible, so I tried the doors on the next landing, they were all closed and none of my hurling of myself at the doors of any help at all, far too strong for me.

This was a dead end for me: suddenly feeling very tired and helpless by the obstructions in my way, plus the loss of blood and all the commotion around me, I decided to go down as a last resort very indifferently, I was just sorry for my Mother if should hear that her son had been shot. I still saw her intense look when she said her good byes, as if to remember me for all time. This was it now, decision without fear descending calmly and reaching the bottom of the stairs.

Wondering which way to go to the front or the rear I noticed a plain clothes Gestapo agent luring from the back door which made up my mind, as he had the door half open now and was slowly raising his luger and straightening the barrel, I put my hands up in the air quickly, claiming to give up but looking him right in the eyes I saw doubt and fear, walking forward at the last moment I jumped on the door holding it and pushed his luger back upwards. He pulled and no shot came out of the weapon. The surmise that there was no bullet in the chamber or that they had forgotten to release the safety catch on both occasions is not for me to analyze.

Was it Russian roulette that had saved my life or divine intervention, my time had not yet come and as the front door gave way under the repeated battering of the rifle butts from the soldiers posted in the street nobody could shoot with me being in the middle and before such a thing was contemplated I was kicked into the street before a line of soldiers whose rifles were pointed straight at me. I found I was the center of their attention and also of the French.

The French people were everywhere, behind the soldiers, jeering them and supporting me like their champion, I felt proud and patriotic, the Germans too were aware of it and I could feel their admiration.

10- Recapture and Sentence:

I was handed over to two uniformed Gestapo, grinning again, they were always doing that. They grabbed my arms and hands and tried to turn them on my back which I resented as they hurt me pushing them far to high, the right one I managed to drag back and out with the strength that was left in it, it was my bleeding hand. I took the lapel of his coat and it got smeared with my blood.

The French onlookers put their arms up and gave me a round of applause. The Gestapo looked at his blood stained coat and swore at me more frustrated than ever now.

That was the best recommendation I could get. I walked proudly back to the Hotel, my hands free just like the general in Eben Elnaille.

Once inside all hell broke loose and all the pent up feelings of these cruel people were released, they- jumped on with me with a sadistic and revengeful unison thumping, beating and pushing me with about everything they could Lay their hands on, from truncheons, belts with "God Mit Uns" and sticks, the ones wearing coats were the worst of all, keeping it up until they were completely out of breath.

I didn't fall down or lose consciousness but instead became senseless to it, every extra beat became very heavy to me. I was beyond pain, switched off. Their amazement was higher than mine at that. I was just dazed and sullen, almost wondering what all the fuss was about. They started telling me that they could have killed me, and that they were such crack shots they aimed at my hand which seems to be very clever considering that I was a moving target.

Also I was congratulated on my bravery, short of awarding me the Iron Cross, they stopped their false flattery and honoring me and the tourist as I call him, pompous about his catch, was ready to carry me off downstairs with the assistance of two soldiers to the converted cellars or dungeons where he gave a speech for the benefit of the inmates of the cells, saying that he would have me shot in the morning as an example to all of them, brandishing his pistol and knocking on the doors so that they could hear him.

I resented his statement of course, and still in the mood of my extreme effort to escape, just in case he felt like shooting me now in his worked up frenzy I thought I had better be ready for any eventuality, so with my back towards him I opened the knife in between both hands and with a backward movement I could have slashed his throat but his three second hesitation to shoot me changed the situation.

Maybe I could have grabbed his luger and started shooting myself getting the prisoners out in the process. It was all in the hands of the gods. He suddenly ordered his soldiers to throw me into the furthest cellar pushing the door sudden open in his hysterical rage. This saved us all from further troubles for the time being. This is how I entered still fuming, teeth clenched firmly, chin forward. I heard the door clanging shut and closing behind me without further ado.

The prisoners surrounded me and jumped back on seeing the knife, Daniel was there as well, everybody had been aware of the escape and the turmoil it had caused. They said a woman had been shot in the erratic shooting and had been wounded in the arm.

Gently they took the knife from me and hid it away. Now with sympathetic understanding surrounding me and the tension of the moment released my adrenalin started dissipating and a sense of feeling came rapidly back, within a few moments I didn't know what to do with myself the reaction being so strong, I was given the only bunk on which to rest and relax.

After what I judged to be about an hour the pain subsided and the Germans said that I was to go, I had to get ready and leave. I just had time to tell Daniel to keep his mouth shut and that was the last I saw of him until the war ended. The knife was used by the prisoners to break out I later heard, this happened after Daniel had gone as well.

I was taken upstairs to the second floor and they put my arm in a sling giving me V.I.P. treatment, disinfectant, ointment bandages and all. They took me to the window showing me the height laughing and saying you certainly won't jump again. Little did they realize I had jumped heights like this before and I was ready to do it again but they held me firmly and the sling was no help either.

Putting me in front of a typewriter and watching me they started the process of interrogation, what they wrote I have not the slightest idea but guessed it to be the worst, very likely to be treated as very dangerous, the only thing they asked was why did I try to escape.

Not to give anything away I said morosely to satisfy them, "Because I was afraid" I didn't want to be shot.

Once a prisoner you couldn't tell them just anything, anyway it was better to be wise and use the point of least resistance. The same evening I was carted off with the first transport put together. Daniel was not in it. As a companion I had a giant of a Corporal who never left my side not for a single minute, that was a bad sign, he even accompanied me to the toilet. I lost my chaperone on arriving at Bordeaux but handcuffs were put on me instead, in fact everybody was handcuffed and with two full vans we were transported through the town. I attempted to wriggle out of the handcuffs, some people can, but it was of no avail, I had intended to jump from the van if so, but it proved to be impossible. Our journey ended at a place called "Caserne- Boudet" an annex of Fort-Du-Ha.

The place was overcrowded, everybody was hitting back at the Boche, and the awakening had taken place. Years of complacency had been disregarded among so many different nation, the best coming to the foreground again determined to get at the common enemy and destroy him.
I was still convinced that they were going to execute me. They must have found out that I was the leader, Daniel couldn't tell them very much about my contacts as he didn't know them either: that was safe in my head. He could however inform them that we were heading for North-Africa or England just by the routes we would have used. I trusted him to keep silent as I would have done. I think the Gestapo didn't persevere, judging us to be unimportant and some of the many they had taken in their big scoop.

So we went on the long waiting list. I was glad of my hand as it seemed to be alright but I was feverish by the time we arrived in a largish hall where they herded us in. The guards were joking around us making signs of the gallows to string us up. This was very demoralizing to us meant to bring our defenses down and torment us.

I didn't like it, mostly because I didn't feel too good and very much enclosed, that hall didn't have much sunlight. The building was old with bars at the top of the curved windows and reeking with the musty smell of age. What a way to go, I thought. I preferred to be executed in the sunlight and open air.

I mumbled something to them and nobody understood me, it was something like a last wish, I must have been really delirious. People pointed to my hand and somehow that explained it to them.
I wished they left us alone now, when we were sorted out they put us in the cells, which were converted rooms with the same curved windows bricked in and bars put in.

I directly thought that this might be a way of escape from the third floor, the bricks in the windows were very loosely and quickly placed, the rooms were quite big containing a lot of people who would be available to help remove the bricks. Those big rooms became my first quarters and the conditions were not very good, one latrine for all of us which had to be carried in and out and cleaned of course, we took turns at this or the senior prisoners, they also dished out the watery soup and rations.

There were some wooden bunks and each of us had a bowl and a metal cup, in that room there were twenty four people. The biggest problem or rather plague was the vermin that swarmed through those buildings.

All kinds and so many that it made one wonder whether they just were poured out from a big bag by Old Nie himself to make life difficult for us or what.

The Germans fully co-operating on this point. From daybreak on the inmates were busy at delousing. At night there was little chance to do that, only when the guards put the light on in short intervals to see whether we were still there and then we heard their heinous laughter like hyenas as they saw us killing the bugs creeping everywhere and stinking from drinking our blood: in the evening we usually put our cups and bowls under the table legs, chairs and beds enabling everybody to have a turn at sleeping on those, the bugs still dropped from the ceiling sensing the warmth of the bodies.

We just couldn't rid ourselves of them, eventually they began to reach the German quarters, however it took time before disinfection took place.

For the moment the Germans enjoyed it, watching us. By the afternoon we managed to get some time for a nap if the guards didn't come and tap the bars, or we were allowed to have an exercise run on the square between the buildings with machine guns trained on us, at the same time we were allowed a smoke from the cigarettes supplied by the Quakers and Red Cross parcels, usually Tjitane and Gauloise, very heavy, real black tobacco.

Some collapsed after taking a quick puff and inhaling in the short time allowed, we found a way to snip the ends off, turn the cigarette around, light it and take a few puffs under the surveillance and satisfaction of the guards, we extinguished the lit end put in a tin and took the best butt end part inside with us making a light when everything was quiet, except for "Donald Duck" who usually could smell it. We used what they called "Amadou ", from coat padding and small flint stones.

Our guards were mostly old reservists pressed into use, Donald Duck was a total non-smoker who noticed the smoke from a long distance and followed the trail standing in front of the door quacking and looking a duck, nobody ever looked more like a duck and sounding like one than him,

He never gave us away either, so no extra punishment was received. His partners were very much the same in their own way, not all ducks. "Yup" was big and stupid always hearing things when there was nothing and vice versa, otherwise, he helped himself to our food parcels and everything else that we possessed.

It was he who replaced my lovely slashing knife with a dirty little pen knife. Incidentally they would never have left that knife in my luggage anyway.

Then there was "Discipline", his pet subject, an old 1914-1918 veteran who had been a prisoner himself placed under Senegalese colonial troops by the French so he had received some bad treatment and undergone trials that he hadn't been to please about either, so we couldn't expect too much quarter from him which he made plain to us from the beginning.

Nevertheless later on when I became one of the seniors in the place giving out the soup, he had us shining the wooden floors with bottles, and however he put the radio on tuned in to B.B.C. and walked away leaving us to listen in.

My hand had healed nicely by this time and I had no after effects from it, I could move it !

The last guard was younger and his name I can't recall but he was very upset one day after returning from leave at home to find most of his family had perished, and he had also been reprimanded before our arrival by his superiors for allowing thirty inmates to escape from the top floor, after taking the bricks away from the window, bending the bars upwards and using their sheets knotted together in strips to get to the street below and flee, in between the patrols and the guard at the gate. Only a few were brought back, the rest got away. So he tapped the bars and watched us like mad. My luck came one day, nevertheless with all caution I nearly did it as it was again with him.

He was just one of those persons, it would take the same course too and this time it would have meant the Russian front for him that was for sure.

It was sheer over prudence now that stopped me now. I had learned my lesson not to be so reckless anymore, on the other hand that is not always the right thing either. One can never tell what would have occurred instead and what one should have done.

It happened so on his shift, one day, we found ourselves cleaning an anti-room out, used as a store room near the street, it had no bars or bricks for that matter built in, good and well shut very dirty, the dust being whirled up with our sweeping so he opened the window for air when at the same time mice disturbed came out from among the furniture as we moved it. Like a cat on the chase he was after them but the mice took off towards the passage way and he was still following them in the heat of the chase now, my mate after them too with me left alone standing straight in front of the window, looking left and right outside I saw just the sentry at the big gate returning, waiting for a chance for him to turn away from my position, my opportunity vanished with the return of my guard who was very flustered and blowing from his run after the mice, looking at me and the window he quickly realized and shut it and that was it, another opportunity I had just missed by running the gauntlet with a lot of bullets ready for the target.

The guard went very red in the face and took us quickly to our rooms ignoring everything else. I bet he had a shock. He wasn't quite sure of anything, neither was I, we had both our regrets, I am sure, for the failure. Such opportunity only comes once, they say.

I remained nine months there and I began to think they had forgotten me as everybody was going on regular transports all before me, there was only a couple like me left. In-between the big room and the soup run I continued my education I should say.

We had nothing else than professors and members of the diplomatic corps left at the end of my stay, who took great delight in teaching us in the evenings and weekends when most of the guards were off duty.

At times like this the guards arranged for us to have the Red Cross and Quaker Packets distributed and we had competitions as to who could produce the best looking cake in the straight bowl, it was a mixture of French bread blended with the ingredients in the packet, from jelly to all kinds of biscuits. It is amazing what came out of it, like that we had an interest and made it last. One poor soul from Lithuania could only hold out for a short while as he was famished, and then he set upon it like a wild animal.

The bugs were still unbearable and I saw one person wrapping himself up like a mummy only to make it worse because they got in between and underneath the material, he had big blobs instead really swollen up to an enormous size and cried like a child, we just couldn't console him, his mind was deranged.

Listening to our Professors talking about Ghengis Khan, Kublai Khan and the light of Asia Buddha brought him back into the fold with us.

Then there was Professor Beck from the University of Tarbes talking about his re-generated potatoes, produced in his Lab: the Nazis were after it also his studies on locusts too started just before the war in Mauretania and Senegal, and of his efforts to make them stay sedentary and produce an ideal food from it, a kind of flour meal. In other words farming locusts.

To top it all there was Maxwell of Brussels talking nine languages fluently and teaching us the rudiments of them all. We even went as far back as Sanskrit with him. There was a real Gypsy amongst us, looking more like a Sikh than any other Indian or Afghan who was taken as such on the frontier in the Pyrenees unable to explain or write in our languages, he was a suspect and they took no chances with him. As a matter of fact the Indian troops left to the south after the B.E.F. evacuation were advised to go towards Bordeaux and made for the Spanish Frontier in a desperate effort to rejoin the British Army, but to no avail. The Germans over ran them and started to implement Gandra Boze's policy on nationalism and collaboration together with the Japanese.

Maxwell was able to converse with our gypsy within a week in his own Romany which was marvelous and started to teach him to read and write in ours. Maxwell disappeared on one of the transports and as he was Jewish there was not much hope for him. At that time I didn't know what happened to the Gypsy but we met again later. Maxwell left us a statement on the real origins of the Gypsies which was only accepted after the war as a proof.

He said that they were an early nomadic tribe from the Punjab regions, travelling westwards towards Europe after the big migrations of de Indo Europeans at a later date. They used the renaissance in Europe to study ancient civilizations in Europe, especially the Egyptians and used the knowledge for their own advantage.

I also met a Polish cadet Janeck who tried to cross the mountains dressed like a Boy Scout which he closely resembled. He had made his way from Poland to Greece over Transylvania eventually to be captured. Later on he told me he had killed a couple of Germans and changed his name from Pareuski to Borofski.

When the Germans caught him in the mountains they let his beard grow for three days and he turned out to be older than the boy he tried to make himself out to be, so that was that for him.
He was on the waiting list too, until they found out more about us all.

One day in a little cell like room I became covered all over with big scabs like Job in the Bible story, lacking in vitamins I supposed, the food, I don't know, the fleas, lice and bug bites gone septic but it took it'time to show up.

The relief and dropping off happened in one night when in my desperation and meditation and on the point of giving up I came closer to God. I felt ready to confess to any priest and ask forgiveness for sins I hadn't ever committed.

We were given time off to see a German Priest in the Chapel across from our cells, closely guarded of course; the man in German uniform gave us a sermon and some asked if he could do anything to help us, to which he responded he would try, but I am afraid the man could do nothing at all, it was out of his hands but he certainly did the effort. With all this my scabs fell off in one night by themselves and what a relief that was, more divine than any priest and traditional taboo could have achieved for me. Divine I believe because in all my efforts to prove it to myself and understand I realized that there was a force at work that stood above it all and everybody was bound to do his duty in it, according to his choice, "To Each his Own".

Everything was coming to an end, we were only a few left. Too many prisoners were uncaught, after the first onslaught. Occasionally we noticed Jewish civilians in the cellars apart; silent and very much to themselves.

One day Discipline took us in a corner of the kitchen, across from the cells, and I could see that there was a way for me to get out of there, the wall was old as in the ancient castle; rather easy for somebody like me to climb, at a slight angle and roughly hewn. As I was studying it I suddenly felt his stare on me, guessing my thoughts, with a little smile on his face he was daring me to try. That would have been alright if I could get away from the inside and had sufficient time to climb unhindered without having somebody like him behind or near to me all the time.

A "Secherheitsdienst" security counter-intelligence of the Gestapo came shortly after that to visit us to see who remained and to peruse our papers. When he returned he looked at my hand and said "that is healed now you can go on transport". We were also inspected as to our general condition and cleanness, very much like any procedure. Discipline was in charge of that telling prisoners very sternly off if he found dirt in any crinkles, like a father figure.

The Protestant Vicar we never saw again, but somehow I think he had a chat with the S. D. man about us.

He was a tall, dark eyed silent type of a man moving in the same mysterious way of mysticism that he portrayed. The S.D. man in comparison looked silent and strict, mostly sharped faced too, a nervous snappy little man in movement and manner.

This person was a prototype of one of the teachers I had known who had turned traitor. Inquisitors and turn coats seem to inherit the same looks and ways of undertakers. Even their uniforms and signs symbolized the dark side of their regime. At the end the only thing he said to us in a shrill croaking executioner's voice: "you lot are due for transportation", first you go to Fort Du-Ha for preparation.

I don't know whether that was better or worse, but going to transportation was something to bring us out of the rut here and maybe another opportunity to jump or roll off the trains, for which we had extensively and ardently trained in the cellars. There was a special way to do this to survive, one had to lay on the footplate of the train with feet towards the engine, gradually rolling outwards and turning quickly into a ball which gave us the best chance, otherwise one had to take the best opportunity available in such circumstances. It also meant, after Fort Du-Ha, that we were still alive and well! How much so that was the question after that!

We departed six months later the same way that we came in, handcuffed, and from Caserne-Boudet annex to the old Fort of Du-Ha built in the time of Cardinal Richelieu.

There was a political section and that is where we were sent and one for criminals with proper separation. We entered through a big ancient gate resembling the entrance of a fortress. We came upon an enormously ugly wide round tower in the center behind which was a square with buildings extending from it in all directions resembling an octopus.

To me that looked like a place of no escape, the bars were thick but flattish, held together by a traversed pair palming the vertical ones in and a wooden box strapped in front of it preventing the prisoners from looking down and drawing attention to a little light coming in from the sky.

The cells were similar to underground vaults, reminding me of old casemates we had found in the woods left around Ostend by the Spanish to stall their horses, very often unearthed by the rains and we used again for hiding weapons. Flush French toilets were added, a convenience not available at Caserne-Boudet. We also had communal showers once a week in the old Tower, walking in a circle.

We had a lot of guards, a small army around us and within the fort. The first cellar allocated to us was on the ground floor and intended to be used to select hostages according to the colored strips on the doors, we later found out. Sometimes we could hear them being taken in the early morning, we also heard brave woman patriots singing the

"Marseillaise" passing by strengthening our moral and pride in the cause. It was all that we had left.

One of the inmates of that cell was a tall thin Southerner from the "Midi" Toulon or Marseilles with a grey patch in his forelock inherited from father to son from generations back. He had been at "Mers el Kebir,"near Oran when the fleet he was in was scuttled by the British resulting in a lot of wounded and dead after the bombardment. He wasn't very glad about the treatment but everybody thought it necessary not to fall into German hands with Darlan.

Sacrifices had to be made, this was going to be our epitaph, unavoidable circumstances. The French indeed had their Daladiers, Petains, Darlans and all very well-known Cagoulards: extreme rightists known for their fascist leanings.

Their deeds surpassed any others, considering the role they played in the first World War, what a pity for this controversy now.

The rest of the fleet the French sunk in Marseilles when the Germans entered un-occupied Vichy, France. Nobody knew what would have happened and obviously they wanted to do it themselves, more so than anybody else.

During the following weeks I was taken to the next floor and lost my brooding fellow and most of my   former inmates. I made new acquaintances and again, met up with Maxwell, an old Spanish Republican Captain, The Gypsy, the young Pole Janeck, Paderwkie and the last new member Zin-Zan, a most unusual name. He came from Eupan-Malmedy the small German cantons ceded to Belgium after the First World War, like the Proctectorates of Urundi and Uranda, annexed to the Belgian Congo as repayment for damages inflicted on us by them.

Zin-Zan was an unknown factor to us, a homosexual and we suspected him of being a ferret planted amongst us. Nothing was said that could incriminate any of us. The food was worse and I don't know what happened to the Quaker parcels that were regularly sent. We had cheese biscuits at the weekends that must have been donated by the Red Cross and they were very consistent but one weekend, due to bad storage, they were hardly edible, so we collected all those that people couldn't or didn't want to   eat, from the cellars, they stuck in your mouth and would have choked you if one didn't swallow lots of water with them. The only thing we could do with them was to stack them all behind the box in front of the bars to air. After a while and having forgotten about them for couple of days "Reiss" the Gypsy tried them again and gladly announced they were O.K. Probably the air and the draught had taken the badness of the mold out of them.

It was like manna from heaven for us, a miracle, we had so many of them we could alleviate our constant hunger a bit.

Maxwell suddenly left us, was dragged out and after that we never saw him again, he wasn't released either. We had a small light table and chairs in the cell and it didn't take too long before we tried the spiritual bit out, our days were long and boring, the contraption worked like mad on the usual questions. I don't know whether it was the tension. How long would we be in prison for and would we live or die. The usual questions one would ask in our predicament. The Spanish Captain was skeptical about his answer, which of course was a negative one. Janeck and mine came to the point where we would meet again on a hill somewhere in the middle of Germany.

The others were saying somebody must have put his foot underneath the table and it was all a bad joke in the worst possible taste. I didn't think that happened at all, but it was better so, because some where getting quite worried about the whole affair and Janeck fully agreed to do better and finish it off.

After that tempers became short and flared up at the slightest excuse and an abstract or evil atmosphere was presently around, it could be boiled down to effect that when people are confined   too long together in a small space tempers become frayed. Or was it something else, a created reaction?

As we took a siesta in the afternoon I was suddenly awakened by terrible screams coming from Zin-Zan, both Janeck and Reiss where masturbating him and we quickly made them stop such practices. The old Captain told them off and Zin-Zan said he was going to call the guards if further attacks occurred. Somehow Zin-Zan got himself out the next day, either he was transported or: Was he really a ferret after all? We were all changed around and lost track of each other shortly after that.

I was put in the last cell of the block on the same floor touching the stairways of the French quarters. Here was an older and more mature group from different walks of life and all from Bordeaux, it seemed. This would top my education and knowledge of this place called Fort-Du-Ha a good deal.

It was the same kind of cell I had left but with a vault hump in the right hand corner near the window side. That is where the stairs were underneath for the French Guards who were contracted out; on the right day we would have a break out when we had found a way to hack through the hump and discover a solution that wouldn't compromise or incriminate the French Guards who would have to be involved in it all.

As it was now, they were feeding us chicken, cigarettes, Lucky Strike, Camels, dropped for the resistance, bread, and meat, saw blades, chisel and hammer, all through the skylight, which was eagerly hauled in. We had long conversations, letters and messages. They could watch the enemy from this lookout easily without being seen.

It didn't take long after entering this cell. I had to be taken in by them and trusted of course, otherwise you were a goner anyway with the people present as they were. We had as top leader there, a man called Carlos, looking like The Sentimental Agent, one of the most and better known entrepreneurs of Bordeux who was supposed to be the son-in-law of Marshal Foch, supplied the Resistance as well as the Germans I believe; then Fischer, a Corsican Police Inspector well in with the Resistance, one of their leaders and also a Councilor of renown for political activities and a genuine Corsican gangster.

Our politician Fiesche was short and strong with a big moustache, the gangster was a James Bond type of man. So we formed a complete set ready for action. Time was all too short for our schedule now and the Gestapo were trying to get us on to transports.

I managed to write a letter and had it sent home by the secret route and it did arrive. My Mother still had it at the end of the war and showed it to me. By that she was able to ascertain my whereabouts, thanks to the Resistance and all helpful souls.

We were planning the time and date of our escape now as we could feel it was more urgent by the minute, every one of us was having an interrogation in turn and who knows what after that.

One day we were nearly caught when one of us was being called out; it was with Carlos I think, by a sullen looking guard as he brusquely opened the door without us having heard him coming or without any pre warning of his approach in any way. We were just having a jolly time regarding our hoard when the door flew open, everything dropping in front of his boots. He just stared at it as if drugged and couldn't believe his own eyes. Lucky Strike packet, matches and all spread out on the floor beneath his feet. In the interval of surprise, one of us, the first was the gangster, managed to kick it under the bed and across, as Carlos was going out he covered the whole scene with a wide gesture and sweep of arms.

Either the guard couldn't believe his own eyes at all or he was seeming to be hypnotized and in a trance or didn't know Lucky Strike from anything else. When the door closed behind him we couldn't believe our luck for the moment.

That would have been the "mittard" or dungeon for at least three weeks for all of us and our escape route blocked because our absence. The dungeons in a fort built in the Middle Ages are terrible things to live in, just a deep pit where you can be completely forgotten, especially by Richelieu. Carlos came back with the news as we had expected, we had to be quick, with no time to lose.

Shortly after him, within the next couple of days, it was my turn to be taken for interrogation.

This was a dilemma, I knew that, fearing the worse I was led to a room near the street in which I noticed the noise of the traffic and could just about see the tramlines. A Gestapo cap and overcoat on, and filling the room with his bulk I noticed what appeared to be a hard or very strong character sitting behind a table with a typewriter on it. Talking to a rather thin raspy looking skeleton of a man, more like a tramp all in all, out on his flat ears, who was desperately and wildly gesticulating with his strong partner. The scrawny one was in plain clothes and drably dressed at that.

When I entered that wretch withdrew, but left the door behind him halfway open, thus reminding me immediately of a previous occasion, not so long ago. I had an instinct for things like that; he was still there watching and waiting on orders to jump in, I could sense that very well. It was a set-up, a trap carefully planned by both and it stunk, I also didn't like the way he had sized me up when I entered, giving me a glance full of hatred.

The stern Gestapo Man told me to sit down now. He began with softening me up and sounded very much like a lawyer combining clever double talk of accuser and defender for my benefit. He told me that I had been locked away for a very long time, away from home and parents, family and friends and if I cooperated with them I could be reunited with them and re-enter society. Would I now like to tell him who were my contacts and where was I going: seriously!

"By the way" he said, "Your friend told us everything anyway" I now knew he was lying because Daniel didn't know anything like that, except that we were going overseas and so did they. So that was too easy. So I said, "It was just a mischievous prank by a mislead youth and that we were going to shoot lions in Africa". At that he lost his temper and smacked me in the face. "You mean shooting German soldiers" he said. I didn't reply to that, that was a bad moment, I heard a slight movement behind me, probably the other one. He was tapping madly on the typewriter and I could feel my face tingling from that smack, he suddenly stopped after thinking and placed his luger on the table within my reach that was it, the moment the other one had waited for too. Never looking up and acting absent minded he now stood up suddenly and turning his broad back towards me walked over to the window, throwing it wide open so that I could hear the traffic below, hooting cars, trams, bicycles passing with bells ringing and people chattering.

Even that in Fort-Du-Ha I hadn't heard for a long time as it was hermetically sealed and thus closed to outside noise. What a temptation did this offer? That was the idea. The devil and his demon: the luger, the chance of a jump, just for the taking, the lamb ready for slaughter and maybe a coffin and hearse waiting. All this was too eagerly and well prepared to take. This was flashing through my mind in a matter of seconds now but another reversal of thinking was saying take it, it's the last chance that you have, you are trained. You know that luger is not loaded, but it is heavy and the weight would make it a good missile, throw it at the living skeleton behind the door, jump your accuser no matter how strong he is and what hidden weapon's he may have and out you go through the window like a bird to freedom or eternity, the trouble was I couldn't fly. I was getting in the mood or a trance if you like with the temptation. It was coming to split seconds, when suddenly from nowhere a small hurricane or inward draught occurred and the windows were thrown or rather sucked shut with a very loud thunder clap which awoke the three of us out of this provoked vacuum atmosphere of foreboding. The figures in this drama started moving again awakened, just like in a scene, a whirlwind of most divine nature had saved me at the very last minute as time was ticking dangerously away for me. Who knows what would have happened there. I am extra strong, I know that, all the Fynaut's have always been, so was my adversary and the poor soul behind me was a wiry little devil on my rear waiting with his pistol at the ready. They saw it was all useless now, I was never going to talk or bend even under torture, I was not the type and would rather die. It was a waste of their time.

In a harsh voice, after having tapped away again on his typewriter and underlining it with red ink, he said to me: "You creeper, will starve in a concentration camp" sentenced to die that was my verdict. Just like the inquisition which it seemed to have copied, that was the ordeal, the last solution. No courts, no justice, no trial of anything!! He called the soldiers and guards to take me back now. I didn't seem to be very impressed, just walked away like to a firing squad, but it was not to be, yet concentration camp, he had said, another chance for me, after all!!

11- Deportation to Auschwitz:

The beginning of 1943 was not too chilly in the regions of Bordeaux, rather more bearable than our cold damp north, a slight ground mist in the morning with lots of sunshine to come for the rest of the day. It didn't look as if our great escape would come to being anymore, any one of us not called up in transport now would maybe gain by the fruits of our efforts and have a chance.

The French guards told us the time was not ripe yet, so I put myself to reasoning that we may never be heard of or seen again and this would be the last place we could report from; everybody else was in the same mood and we left our memories on the walls like prisoners do, inscribed.

I put the most innocent addresses that couldn't recriminate anybody while the Germans were still there, so I put my family addresses in England. Later towards the evening nearly everybody knew about the fact that we were due for transport, and the news was such that the allied landings were imminent, so the Germans wanted to get us on the way, far away.

By the evening a hell of a racket was heard from all the cells in the whole of the fort in unison, singing and pots banging together. Then the Germans, from the centre yard assembled and gave orders over a megaphone that they were going to start shooting in; the din gradually subsided to nothing. The next off morning we were all called to be to the ready and then cashed/with some meagre food distributed just in advance of departure. Transportation army vans brought us all to the station in intervals until we were all gathered up, there was quite a lot of involvement there. S.S. in the rear wagons with soldiers and the least of all, collaborators and lots of plain clothes police, all heavily armed.

Our inquisitor - Gestapo - was there too, the strong one. When the convoy was complete we were all pushed in the goods wagons, the two end spaces left for us and the middle section reserved for two soldiers with a sergeant, the sliding doors were left open, no facilities for ablutions, the sections were divided with two strings only. In this manner we departed from Bordeaux.

The only chance I saw for possible escape was when we passed over the big river Gironde, on a high bridge, but as the train was rolling steadily along, the pylons came in to quick a succession to be able to make a jump for it from under the strings and out of the open doors into the tempting water we could   see from far below us.

After this we tried with what turned out to be a Belgian pilot called "Allard" from Leige to persuade the others to make a break for it in unison. Jump the guards in the wagon could be easily done before they could draw their weapons. To unhook the wagons at the rear with the machine guns covering both sides we both volunteered to do: soon we found out it was not possible. The mixed sections from a very assorted crowd, old ones some tortured to the point of incapability, but most of all the majority were to apathetic for such an ongoing action. The majority of those people wouldn't come back, neither would "Allard" Much later I saw his photo for the missing displayed after the war in one of those big multiple panels. The Gestapo had thought of all the most possible ways and means. The long journey went on for a good way until the S.S. and Gestapo thought it was time for a relief stop, somewhere in a field ideally situated, to take place and also strategically covered to shoot any would be escapees down.

I had my inquisitor coming closely near me and keeping an extra watchful eye as I was indeed looking at my chances near the wheels and a bit further away from the crowds. I guessed the Guard was thinking I might make a try to escape as underneath the wagons I could see the open field, to reach the coverage of the trees in the distance was too much of a run so I took my trousers off and showed what I thought of it all to my Gestapo man. I cannot judge his immediate reaction to that but I thought he displayed a slight human kind of smile. I also knew he was an excellent, well trained shot, my logic told me that. My intuition told me more also to wait for a better opportunity than this one. I couldn't trust his misleading reactions at all.

When this episode was over, Allard and I tried to study the trap windows in the corner, under the cover of our inmates, we had a knife to work at it. It was a bit high and it had to be done with the advantage of darkness and silently and then to drop at the other side with the speed and nearness to the wheels, which would certainly draw you underneath them!

Nothing came of it, the drop was too high, close and awkward. In this manner we carried rolling on until we reached Compiegne. One might as well say, that all roads seemed to lead to Compiegne instead of to Rome. The usual groups of lots of young German soldiers this time were waiting for us and we were escorted by them through the town. The inhabitants were looking on what for them must have been a common occurrence by now. No way for us to run between those detained youngsters either, they seemed to be to experienced and too much on guard by the look in their eyes underneath their formidable helmets, hanging deep on their heads making a trap for those that knew it; it was a look of total possession, obsession and dedication. The indoctrination had done its work very thoroughly on them. We were the absolute baddies for them and they were definitely the ultimate baddies for us. This was what total war had brought us to.

After passing a higher elevation and open fields it was a relief after being inside various places for so long, for myself I had lived for nine months in this manner.

We entered the trial-camp where they sorted us out for unknown transportation, most certainly to be Germany. We had a look around at our situation and lost our liberty which was outside the barbed wire fence, lots of fresh air and water to wash, not too much to eat, even though we were given some work to do. Meeting old and new acquaintances, it was more like a prisoner of war camp. The Allied landings were on everybody's lips and near to fruition but most of it a lot of wishful thinking and hopes, which made the Germans pretty nervous at times. They already had a basin full with the daily waves of Allied planes flying over us on their way to Germany heavily loaded. Super Fortresses by day, R.A.F. by night. The U.S.A. was involved in the war by now. This knowledge was a great support to us knowing that the Germans were tied down on the Eastern front and in retreat.

Some work was handed out in the camp regarding the ruble of some buildings that were being demolished and I noticed the bricks being loaded on two old Polish farmers carts pulled by horses and only two old German guards. I thought maybe there could be another possibility occurring to get into the cart and let the inmates, with that knowledge, cover me up with bricks and once out of the gates, after a short span time, to get out from the rear at the right moment when the guards or rather the two drivers weren't looking, as they seemed to be more like two old village elders. So I volunteered for it but the Polish supervision couldn't be trusted I found out to my consternation, or at least I thought so.

Tunneling out was also considered but nobody stayed long enough even to start on it or form an escape committee. A Belgian survivor from Blakenberghe came back one day with the tale of some escapes from the trains before reaching the German Border but he said it was sheer slaughter, most of them got killed.

We had arrived at Compiegne on the 1st of April and stayed for one month only, this had given us enough time to pick up and improve our health and clean our clothes; once again we were gathered for transportation no respite, not without taking our numbers up and respective cases indicated, all this was specially sorted out as to which destination we had to go to as judged and marked on the Gestapo files. For that we were provided by a number going from one to three next to our names.

We tried to make out the severity of this numbering but as we were all in the same transport we were painted with the same brush, or even better than that we were branded like cattle. One of the famous nominations we came under was "N.N:" or the "Nacht and Nabel", the night and fog destination, those who had to disappear silently without trace. We waited the whole night through in a cold brick building just sitting against the wall dozing.

There was a bright full moon and I remember I had a sinus headache with a chill. The following morning it was better, because from now on one could forget about any treatment or relief. You just had to grin and bear it for better or worse with greater suffering to anticipate more often than not. After being marched off we were herded back in a repeat performance and pushed into overfull goods wagons just off the rail tracks of the station, in a very isolated place and we were all given a special sausage which was treated with some chemical to dehydrate us, soon after eating it we found that out, the speedy elimination process had started now.

The crush in the wagons was so tight we had no room to sit down, everything was hermetically closed, no toilets and just before pushing the doors shut on us, like in a big coffin, a tall German Officer S.S., thin and stalky like a beanstalk with a face to match it and the eternal self-imposed grin: screeched "Bon Voyage" and with a big gesture slammed the doors on us drawing and clanging the bolt. That's exactly how it must feel to go to the slaughter house. The train began to roll steadily along and we quickly got the trap doors open, a little at a time in our corner, for more air, somebody always had a knife and as in our case, pencil and paper. It was time to drop and pass messages before we came to near the border and we were still a bit perky. It was the twenty sixth of April, 1944.

We figured the transport to be circa at one thousand eight hundred men, and we had not the slightest idea where we were going - "Quo Vadis", one hundred and twenty per wagon, some were bigger wagons than the others, nothing to drink or eat just that terrible sausage, which we soon learned not to touch, some did so in desperation, but we all had tried some of it before of course.

With a bit of luck we managed to get numerous messages out and with a bit more luck they would be picked up along the way which was followed by the resistance members who walked along after any transport. So good, our train got the attention somehow and was followed all the way during its four day journey I believe from the air. Before we crossed the German frontier we were counted with sticks and the bashing team going at it together in great force. They really let go, some prisoners that weren't quick enough at jumping out and back in received gashes on their heads that were deep and they bled profusely, a real pity to look at them; the S.S. here were assisted with some added German police. This was to make sure there were no escapees on their hands, the mad counting and the bigger complement of guards, and as we were now in Nazi Germany looked like a kind of Welcome Society showing what they stood for as a matter of fact, an experience never to be forgotten for those that would come back.

Now the continuous rolling and the terrible stink and mess of our confinement started to take its toll. Standing like sardines in a tin we had to make room somehow. Some must have been lying on each other or sitting between each other's legs, also a place had to be made for people to relief themselves. At some stations, when the situation got too bad, and after hearing the crying for water, some foreign workers passed in cups of water and we all had a couple of sips from it, in turn, in my wagon. I don't know about the others, some didn't.

One of the old fellows which I vaguely recognized from the Bordeaux transport, looked at me pitifully, he had a big weeping infected cut on his head and with his wide open eyes told me by look, you were right, we should have escaped on masse when our strength and means were at their best. I was continuously thinking the same thing too.

Things were becoming awfully remote now as the train moved on. The mentioning of the word "Shweinhunden" I had first heard when the counting took place and was now far behind us.

What was the next thing in store? It didn't take long as we kept rolling along. We heard the waves of airplanes overhead and the flak but nothing near enough happened to bomb us, which we more than half wished for, never mind the causalities, it was a chance.

This was the best that could befall us, I think, no such luck, we kept rolling on till half-way through Germany, as then I figured out we must have been somewhere in Prussia, by now.

We came to a long stop maneuvering backwards until we were out of the way and waiting again along the side track.

Indifferent by now we couldn't care more or less. Somehow no room was found for us there and the tracks had to be kept free and the dying had to be kept on, so after a while we moved towards the East.

We found out that the sausage that had been given to us must have contained a lot of sodium, or something similar.

Through the opening we started noticing names like Leipzig, so most likely the stopover must have been and was Weimar. Chemnitz began to show up the following day and coal heaps with depressing drab looking towns in Polish Silesia rose up in front of our look-out.

I tried to work out where we were heading for, the salt mines of Wieliczka maybe, I heard so much about it by the Belgian political prisoners of 1914, or maybe the Russian front to dig trenches, we desperately hoped.

This was much unknown territory for us, that far East. I started feeling ill with stomach cramps, damn that sausage, it was also hunger and all the rest by now, plus a terrible thirst. There were only a few people still standing up around me talking turns in doing it to get some space. One of them started rubbing my stomach to relieve the pain. After that I fell asleep for a while, an uneasy sleep with dreams of running water from reservoirs over dams and weirs in between them, containing very nice clear cool fresh water. Now the thirst was becoming a problem more than anything else. The space in the wagons was minimal and to stuffy to breathe properly.

I was abruptly woken by cries and noise outside, the train coming to a long halt and sudden stop. Noise and a tumult of short orders, doors flung open, one after the other, till it came to ours and the shouting and ordering of "Er rausch", get out, I didn't notice the "Shwainhunden" bit but it must have been there too, continuously by now, one gets quickly accustomed to being treated like an animal. We were total wrecks, unshaven, bewildered, sick, frustrated, indifferent and completely disorientated by now. That's the way they wanted us to be!

The biggest part of that was all carefully planned and calculated with what they called a proficient German efficiency program.

Murder incorporated was waiting for us in mass. All sorts of S.S. fighting and political units from the tartars, welcoming us with an authentic and theatrical bit of real Teutonic reversed charm. Whoever amongst us still had any doubts they would be gone within a few seconds all dreams of any compassion were dashed to pieces. The S.S. all had big grins, to compare it with hyenas would be an insult to the animals, I think. Anyway they were there in full force, ready to begin their lugubrious work as a business.

What transpired now one had to be there to believe it, and even then it's hard to comprehend?

Whilst we started gathering and still some being carried out from the wagons by their mates I had a quick side glance at the enormity of the camp and its far extensions afar. From where I stood I couldn't see the end of it on my left side at all. The security fence appeared to be double barbed with the outer electrified, once in there you were certainly well secured, no expense seemed to have been too much. I had a quick glance at some of the inmates nearest to us, now. Women and men, I couldn't see any children. All dressed up ready for an enormous ball or carnival, moving along like zombies, some carrying between them on two long poles a big barrel dangling in the middle.

It was more than enough to see, the threatening S.S. drew my attention now. A tall grinning skull and crossbones S.S. officer shouted at the wagon occupants to bring out the wounded and half dead near to him and he stood legs spread out on what looked like some woodpiles nearby about twenty feet away, facing the whole miserable herd in length and breadth of our column as seeming to have descended from Dante's Inferno. He was gesticulating and waving his long arms with a luger in his hand in every direction possible. He might as well have had no uniform or flesh on his body, Death itself!

The wounded all still very much alive pulled along by the S.S. soldiers and spread out at his feet, some begging, I do not know for what, feeling death too near I suppose, and pointing his luger at us in a sinister way, laughing he began to shoot the lot of them, twenty to twenty four, one at a time in the head some in the neck still hysterically laughing more and more now. When he had finished he just went on laughing again, as though he enjoyed the whole game tremendously, he probably did so to impress all of us. We just stood there perplexed as though we had arrived in another hell hole, which was another inferno being stoked up for us, beyond any credibility. A French Officer, a few paces from me, detached himself from us giving the usual gesture as if he was going to relieve himself, but about twenty feet from our end of the column stood an S.S. motorbike. A German policeman was in between and slightly sideways wondering what that Frenchman had in his mind at that moment. The man kept on coming on so that the S.S. officer noticed it and screaming loudly to the police said "shoot him quickly he is after my bike". At this the policeman shot him in the leg, just at close range which made the Frenchman tumble in his length backwards; he got up again and now putting his arms up for the surrender sign. The S.S. still storming forward in a rage now, howled to the police to shoot him and they shot him in the heart. When he did that in hesitancy it was the Coup de Grace to finish it off. Somehow this had taken the breath away from the S.S. Officer, all the effort and excitement, and he had had enough of it; a pause for us.

The burly younger hooligan S.S. soldiers took over from there and mumbled from their corners obscene, blistering ghoulish remarks to us: "Funeral March".

An open van had arrived with senior inmate prisoners gathering the well expected harvest of cut down bodies and throwing them like sacks of potatoes on this van, very much similar to harvest time, all very casual and usual. We were pushed and bullied around to form ranks of five and to give each other an arm, it made it easier for them to watch us, like that.

After this performance the march started with the van and victims leading, under close surveillance for me and Janeck, who I found just behind me in the next row, a bit too close for safety.

A bully of an S.S. Officer and his mate were marching alongside and we were also to near the front for my liking, ready for the first repercussions they would take on any looseness according to their views. For one moment I thought this was going to happen as we proceeded to the left turning the corner of the camp place. The hulk said to his companion an S.S. Soldier, motioning towards our direction: "I think one is going to break free here", putting his hand on his hip all ready to pull out his pistol. Luckily for us whatever it was that made him do that the moment passed. As we marched down the electrical barbed wire towards a small row of trees full of Carrying Crows making a din and screeching, reminding one of vultures gathering: some circling around and swooping down in an erratic long swift glide, croaking and fluttering, making a remarkable spectacle for the approaching column. No other birds were present in the pale sky and one was aware of an atmosphere of disaster and utter despair around us.

It was quiet and oppressing, almost close to noiseless. The column of death kept on relentlessly, moving along that muddy dirt road in Poland.

Coming out of the woods the first thing we saw in the distance was the foothills of the Karpathos. Of course immediately dreaming of getting to those hills with the first opportunity.

Still very thirsty and dry but now at the back of our minds, from the gruesome reception that the welcome committee had laid on for us, I got the illusion of babbling cool mountain streams around me with dark green grassy meadows that I could drop into and be cajoled into lusty frolicking games.

In the meantime the S.S. Officer and soldier had moved forward, giving Janeck and me an opportunity to talk with him moving close to me to do so. On our left grotesque and behind the barbed wire a couple of weird looking buildings appeared quite large in size, at least thirty to fifty feet long and twenty five wide, looming up in our wide eyed view. One side had barred windows but the other small rectangular openings that could be hermetically sealed again, and was the thickness of a safe. The side that had the windows was also provided with long bars.

Janeck pointed them out before I could ask him, "Is that where we are we are going to work?" He quickly responded "Don't be silly", being more with it and up to date he said, "Those are gas chambers and crematoriums". They were all in one system, newly constructed and maximum one year old at the most.

12- Auschwitz:

As a matter of fact this was still hard to swallow for us, but there it was in all its glory in actual fact. It couldn't be clearer now and better represented as it unfolded itself perfectly to our opened eyes. One shock followed the other in rapid succession now since our arrival to this and the next one as we kept on marching. We were still alive less twenty five people. Our mood which was very down became even more somber by the minute.

It was the end of April when we set out and now it was the second of May 1944. Nobody had heard of this hidden extermination camp yet, all this was very much incognito. Nevertheless after the war, and during this period of time, they showed us aerial photographs of people standing in a queue waiting their turn at those Gas Chambers. Why not bomb the whole place completely? What were the odds for all of us? After the Jews it was us, anybody under the slightest suspicion, those considered as "*untermensch*" they would have made *"lebensroum"* just for themselves and enough slaves left over to serve them in turn for this.

This scheme was far too big and well organized with the other grotesque ideas in mind to be just for religious, ethnic, or enemies of their thousand years "Reich" final solutions.

The weather at this time was still very humid and cold with waterlogged flat land. On arrival when we were still with the wagons, well behind us now, we had also noticed a little sharp church steeple to the North West of us some distance away which some time later I learnt that it was Birken au village. We also noticed that those ghastly buildings had a tall square tapering chimney in each center, they were not smoking at the time. Passing those burning houses for Molloch I should say where they used to throw the first born and sacrifices in like the prisoners and other victims of old, this was very much on the same scale considering the modern mass production against the ancient land of Canaan with its open fires and ovens. The reality was too striking.

We finally came to a halt at a big gate, hell's gate. Our luggage followed, the dead in front and the living in the middle and behind as left overs. Entering this gate which was opened wide and under close surveillance we were stopped and gradually led into what looked like a sorting building long and low: called "Kanada"; by the numerous working inmates nervously rushing around to be ready to receive the orders from the S.S. standing in mass around, some with dogs. All our belongings were being sorted and passed along the human assembly line, including even what we had on except for our belt, which for the moment was still a good sign as we were to be outfitted with other clothes.

The destination of our clothes was "Wintershelp" for the Germans, needed, including for the soldiers on the Eastern Front. The Gestapo bureau was a lucrative business and a well-oiled enterprise with so much of the state under its complete control too, being a state within the state. No other organization known was so much in charge of everything and feathering its own nest at the same time. No Mafia or old established order had come so near to this in such a short span of time with so much crime dispatched and displayed with utter complete enjoyment. Murder incorporated had never come as near to anything as this. To our further amazement an S.S.was going over our files with numbers again, contemplating the orders of our fate was a big round faced S.S. Which very much later I recognized as being the bully that was Kramer, the well-known butcher of Sacksenhausen concentration camp. With his dog close to him, shaking his head continuously to some of the Jewish helpers, called "der sonder-commando" or the sin commando, so named because they survived by doing the burning, the hard labor and dirty work, usually for another extension on their life, if lucky, for a further six months, then to be replaced and in turn to be candidates for the Gas Chambers. They helped to put their own families and other people in and also pulled them out to be cremated in the powerful ovens. All this was told to us by their own while we were waiting: there also seemed to be a lot of complications, orders and counter orders going back and forth in a somewhat oversubscribed communication system around us. It was even suggested that we shouldn't be there at all, we were in the wrong place and accommodation should be made ready with the idea of moving us out again as quickly as possible, the ones that had got so far, in that way we wouldn't see too much whilst there. Still N.N. under the disappearing numbered. To be shot directly if we went slightly out of line. This turned out to be very much so, I had gone inside and lost track of Janeck, everybody was busy looking after himself, I should say, in contemplating how to attack as a last resort.

I had decided from the middle of the pack as nobody would move in the forward position. I was halfway down sitting against what we were told were showers, but the concrete boxes looked like two fold contraptions to me, big thick doors again, dark cellular looking inside with a pipe sticking out from the ceiling. Maybe they were disinfecting chambers for the clothes, but foremost we were told they were old gas chambers, the first old building used for this, the stable they called it. I worked out that they could maybe take ten or more people, and there were about three or four of them as far as I could see.

I didn't look to closely, don't forget we were still in a state of dehydration getting worse by the minute, some had drunk from the water on the ground which was dirty and disease ridden. Rushed orders came suddenly and we started moving, I left the dammed doors quickly and hurried into the queue to be shaven.

On an elevated platform were different prisoner barbers shaving us crudely with blunt and rusty razors on every hair they could find. We came out of this ordeal scratched and bleeding: a fairly large Jew from Antwerp, better dressed than the others, explained to us all the ins and outs, the daily routine of the camp and what we should keep. Having passed him at last every batch was assembled in a larger place with security at both ends, big sliding doors, one young S.S. was waiting halfway inside controlling valves, which was for the water lucky for us, which he did so after having let about twenty of us in at the time, he opened some valves and a few drips came out from the pipes above us which we drank eagerly looking stupidly at each other for more and then at him; at that moment a tumult arose on my left and near the corner closest to me, approaching it I saw there already some people near, and as the S.S. was coming too, swearing like hell now, I kept my distance.

One prisoner had tried to cut his wrist with one of the old razor blades he had been able to obtain. With the belts a tourniquet was wound around his wrist and the S.S. furiously told him off saying that he couldn't do so without his permission and how stupid he was. That fellow must have been Simon Wiesenthal, anyway he survived and came all the way with us, and they never noticed or separated him from the rest of us. He wasn't allowed to take his own life, what a sarcastic twist of the whole chicanery.

They were going to take our lives away when they felt like it but even that had become their prerogative.

Obviously they thought the only real authority was from the abyss, the oath they had taken said so.

Before we passed through the opposite door we received a complete immersion in a concrete trough filled to the brim with a green liquid that could have been a kind of disinfectant, as somebody put a heavy round mop on our head like a plunger dipped in the same stuff. It was like a baptism, away from this glorified treatment we found ourselves in a long draughty corridor in which we had to run its length.

You can imagine as it was night, cold and early in the year we were only too glad to make a good run for, it felt near to freezing point. Chilled to the bone now, and still having that sausage with us that we couldn't eat, we had had nothing to eat or drink. I think five days had passed by now and we lost track of time.

At the end of the hall we came to a room full of clothes spread out and you just chose the ones that fitted best, as well and as quickly as one could. These were full of bullet holes, a dried red and covered with lime on them but all quickly prepared in what looked like their old gas chambers. So we put them on looking like very sorry clowns, similar to the people we had seen running around. Even in our state we couldn't help to release a pitiful laugh when looking at each other and some poking their fingers through the holes, still as in disbelief.

It seems to me in a situation such as this most minds can only take so much and then it stops or snaps altogether. You just keep going on, after what I have just reported, I have today people of all walks of life telling me after witnessing it with my own eyes, that as I didn't see all the rest but heard of it with my own ears on the spot and observed even the aftermath on some of my fellow prisoners, who came with the lugubrious news back to us, after wishing themselves to be as far away as possible if they did return, that it was still difficult to comprehend or convince themselves that such things could happen.

I didn't actually see the people being pushed into the death houses and gas chambers but witnessing the fact is just as difficult in trying to convince a reversed and indoctrinated media and flat world believers as Galileo had found out through the centuries.

To what extent one can go in disbelieving is dependent on the impact of the reverse force. Our liquidators were masters at it, covering up their atrocities and murders; but the results spoke for themselves. All this is fathomless and incomprehensible. We'll never understand the whole of this affair spiritually or otherwise, how it was made possible.

Even the S.S. didn't act as if they did it themselves and it was almost as if it was a favor and they could forget the whole affair just as quickly as they had done it and it never existed. So much was never understood from those that had never been there, what the use of us was being there then, unfortunately we happened to be there anyway, a result of what they called a war they had forcibly pushed on us and all.

To tell the truth as we saw it and then to be told, or near enough, it could not be so, seems to be almost the same situation as we now find ourselves in in today's society.

At this rate it is very difficult to prove anything at all; maybe it could be boiled down to a bad dream, life and death is only a passing event. The S.S. proved that given backing and power they could do anything to anybody like the wild animals, from the small infinite viruses to the big catastrophes, earthquakes, floods etc.

The belief and faith that the all being suddenly decides at a certain point it is enough and you can walk through the Red Sea or any other way destroying your enemies at the same time is a very strong faith or suddenly one individual will be saved among all the dying chosen from all the others like an ant that is not trodden on. Such things did happen but for the majority it didn't, everything went by clockwork. The trains went to their destinations on time, the gas chambers worked excellently and nothing came in the way of the smooth flow of affairs put into motion, people accepted their death as a matter of fact near the end, no doubt. And if you didn't it made absolutely no difference. One was not capable of doing anything else but suicide. Soldiers were dying on all fronts from all sides and we must include the civilians that were bombed. Only time would overcome with superior powers and this stopped the total destruction which enabled rebuilding and a normal return to life for the masses.

The creator was in all this, somehow, but who knows his way of working, cleaning the culmination of all the wrongs with more and better wrongs. The passing of events we really did not understand but the visible things are just there for the living and it is the same with the whole universe and its workings. You can see it.
Beyond that we just don't seem to know or comprehend the infinite whole, however much we try to figure it out. The spirit challenges even against its own maker. Everybody think he has the monopoly over what? Until ground down to nothing over and over again.

In no time at all our little groups came out in the cold moonlight, silvery and spooky to us hanging over the camp giving its reflected light over this side of the globe and its creation of doom and gloom.

We had little wooden soles with canvas over our feet and a little bit of a kind of bread crust received. I don't know anymore, sometimes I don't remember every detail and I dread that amnesia would make me forget most of it by desire for not wanting to know or think anymore; my real conscious nature has a great ambition to discern the truth more than anything else.

Until we were reassembled the whole transport was pretty well intact I should say. Twenty five missing was nothing yet on what we contemplated was to come because we couldn't see it all only the knowledge of the sky and stars at night and by day the sun, clouds and light, the feeling of cold and warmth, pain and sorrow, at this point we were nearly senseless.

All those things we knew, they were still present but we didn't see the results of the events leading up to it, it was obscured, very much so, we could just about see the atrocities and the cruelty and we were still alive, somehow, otherwise some survivors wouldn't be here either to tell the truth. If you got too much out of line you were just shot or pushed or walked into the gas-chamber yourself, with the pushing or pulling what's the difference. There was no other way that I know about that can be emphasized enough for the disbelievers, my cup is dry from here on.

We moved like Les Miserables, trying to walk with those planks on our feet, lots of people today think that it's good for your feet, humbug, but we had to get used to them immediately and the earth was very wet and marsh like, I think this place was constructed on the moors to make it harder to endure. Having walked inside now and passed the two impressing Frankenstein buildings with their smoke stacks standing out in the bright moonlight as clear as Cleopatra's needle or obelisk, I sighed and thought we are too close to those things for my own safety.

All those barracks long and dreary looking without windows were mostly on the right now from us and the two last ones on the left next to the furthest crematorium they put us in, with all the time guards backed up with extra reinforcements, strict orders were given not to leave the barracks at all, there was one latrine outside next to it with a long pit alongside also with water coverage in different places inside. That was all, no bunks, no chairs, no tables, condemned people sentenced to die do not need to sit or lie down.

They are just allowed to drop. There was still no drinking water so most of us drank of the dirty pools on the earthen floor with dire results to follow. I abstained and found myself a place against the back of another fellow or alternatively against the wooden panel as people started dropping again and making room in this way. I put one sole under my buttocks, the other under my feet, in this way I took some naps in the long and eventful night that followed. Firstly I was rudely awakened by a couple of shots, some of our fellows got shot for daring to go outside for starters, so that was out of bounds.

Later in the night we heard muffled voices and shoveling which we couldn't make out why, as we couldn't see anything, you see, we were always left completely in the dark. The morning of another day arrived and we were allowed to go in the early dew to the pit managing for what we had to do.

The two shot bodies of our comrades were placed next to the pit to be hauled away. When the food came around which was at nine, judging by the sunlight, that I am afraid I cannot really prove either, not having an instrument to give us a measure of standard time which I say we accept as a matter of fact. Sometimes a machine made by man and programmed to his conceptions is more believed than man himself. This is again especially the case today and I have noticed the dis or unbelievers have a special attraction to these things, as that is something they can see and even argue with which I have observed to my utter amazement, but not unbelief like them.

A knowledge of time was gotten somehow by us, the soldiers had watches but it was safer to keeps ones distance from them. After the bodies had been removed and the soldiers had left, don't forget we were in a camp within the camp, we noticed and found ourselves to be in between barbed wire on the inside of an electrical fence.

The food was atrocious, but food that we eagerly ate, just a bowl with a glue some jellylike substance holding the cabbage and some seeds together, I think it was some Rye. No utensils of course, a little bread was provided and we managed to pick up with that and slurping the rest like animals do, that was the idea, we were reduced or rather brought down to that level.

After this we took our positions and talked a bit, we could see farther afield in between the buildings.

The camp had come alive and there was a lot of movement and the short snappy noises of shooting mostly pistol shots was heard from all over and especially from the direction between the barracks.
Some of us had to explore a bit closer and they didn't return except for one full of terrible stories telling us with wild staring eyes, the S.S. were shooting nonstop infants and babies placed and held on chairs.

I don't think we could envisage anything worse anymore, just thinking this is what happens in this camp although our feelings and judgment of such a happening were of utter disbelief and comprehension. Because of this I was determined to make a last stand, when I looked around I could find no similar response from my fellow prisoners for it. What was the matter? They were not active like comrades in arms at all, just very sullen sheep to become shot or put to the sword.

What had happened while people were put into the big gas chambers and ovens you might well ask, nothing! You have to wait like us standing there, hearing and observing, afterwards wondering where all the people had gone to. For this purpose those ovens were made ready for bigger fry.

Later in the evening we had the first glimpse of the new arrivals in two big transports similar to ours, which appeared to be in great haste. They were placed in the opposite barracks, women, men and children all Jews from Hungary. The Eichman program had started on the Reich's and his declaration of the final solution for them. Direct and total dissemination, no pause at all.

The fires were waiting and stoked to the full. Lots of new fresh human fat, hair and ashes, it all had its uses too, as well as anything else.

We were put in our barracks again, safely out of view, with a 24 hour guard on us and not the slightest movement was allowed nor a quick peep near the doors was permitted, many of the inmates had learned the lesson the hard way.

All through the night we heard shuffling, muffled cries and weeping, interrupted by the shouting of the S.S. here and there. Death itself was among us, it was him walking the perimeter in whatever form or shape you may wish to give him an angel or devil if you like, it was all around. You could hear it, think it, and feel it, almost see it, mostly by sense, because we can think it, even animals are aware of that. It is there present as thick as a large dirty bog full of skeletons and it stank of human flesh.

Already the column for mass slaughter was moving towards the fires, an endless ribbon of human misery and a tragedy we kept on hearing it, and at last when morning came after an uneasy sleep in which nightmares would have been completely unnecessary as reality was even worse. The guards left, their mission completed now and we went out into the blinding sunlight and, Oh my God! We looked at the chimney stacks, they were smoking bulging big fires close to their top, finishing off with thick fat oily smoke rising high in a ball like formation and then curling off into one direction, driven by the wind, over the damp landscape spreading far out to dissipate into nothingness.

This was the people we had heard and all that remained was ashes. This time there were tears in our eyes, believe me, we stood there watching it and there was nothing we could do about it in our incapacity of complete dissolution, not even one grey uniform was to be seen around now, just us.

We stood with clenched fists, lost in our own thoughts, hopeless. We looked at the billets, empty and again a terrible feeling of desolation. No life in it at all, not the slightest sign, absolutely nothing, just us.

On the barracks double gates were big boards with notices of cholera and typhus written on it, the great lie, and so what, we knew that they came in alive. The boards were for our bene fit, to make us believe we had imagined things and not seen or heard anything and it was just a fumigation procedure.

It is beyond me how this action could be explained; the S.S. were half mad themselves to go through such a procedure.

We spent another night in that hollow spectacular place with those events ever present which we were supposed to have never seen there. The chimneys still kept on smoking for a long time, like a church organ puffing out a tune which eventually slowed down to a regular beat. Whoever would believe this as an epitaph of the people? This was more than any show that could be produced. A factory with an assembly line to mass produce killings well-conceived in its entire operation, running exactly as it should, smoothly and on time. Who couldn't equalize anything with that?

It aggravates ones thinking if there is any "justice" when it is to be found in this whole project of injustice.

We have failed abysmally, we are not capable of running things right, the wisdom is awfully lacking if that is possible. We were moving away from this gory sight always moving further inside, but separate from the Jewish sections which we could see all of them around us.

As I have already said, we had about thirty of their people amongst us hidden and let through, nobody had squealed or showed they noticed. By looks or circumcision, even some of us could be looking like some of them, such was the world of two thousand years of living amongst us not completely void in many instances of looking like each other.

We were given better bunks, one blanket, a heated floor through the center constructed of brick and looking more like an ancient Roman drain.

We had more drips of water, a bit in Compiegne and in the open air, cold and Spartan. Food was brought regularly to us, the same brew in huge barrels carried by the Hebrew slaves to us.

On morning and evening roll-call we were made to watch how they ill-treated our Jewish inmates opposite and a bit further along from us.

On such an occasion we saw one day the Commandant of the camp which was Mengele, and also his beautiful camp companion from about fifty yards away. It was a show for our benefit, they were beautiful specimens however with a whip in their hands giving orders to other Capo prisoners or the supervisors to beat any other prisoner up, they pointed out some imaginary disorderly conduct that they thought fit for punishment with a horsewhip. They told one to lie down exposing his back and beat him up with a last kick to get up and join the ranks again, for this special event. This was on the order of the day, the prisoners told us.

We were now at the eleventh day not knowing what would happen to us, doing nothing, we had a weekend over and still alive in the camp when we heard the music of some sort of band floating on a feeble wind, it was the marching into gas chambers music. More and more of us became very sick, very ill actually, the drinking of the dirty water maybe and other diseases starting to take their toll very heavily amongst us.

We also heard the shooting further all the time but away from us now, we couldn't see too much, kept well away I should say, from the scene, we came to know it by the other inmates that the band was used to walk the inmates to the old gas chambers near the stable. I couldn't actually tell you whether we had been in it exactly either when we first arrived or what, but that's what we thought somewhere there, we heard the noise and what they were. So even being there we found ourselves always in doubt at any given moment.

We were told we were due for transport and to be ready and when the day and moment came we were led out of this center to the other side of the camp and there we saw more crematoriums with gas chambers, which we hadn't seen before, all in all there must have been some five chimney's as later described.

Turning the corner slowly we saw some Jewish girls near their own circled fences and further away, lots of Jewish children playing like on any other school grounds or playing fields. They even started throwing bread to us and speaking in French saying they came from Lille, northern France.

Somehow somebody put the question to them, "what do you think will happen to you"? In unison they looked at the crematoriums and chimneys, pointing to them and said "That's where we are going soon", shaking their heads up and down in one accord they knew and had no doubts, even smiling in a sure way, well aware of the short time left to them to live, we looked more frightened and worried than them as anybody would have. We were shouted at to move, and quickly they cried to us, hanging with their little hands on the fence: "Tell the world please, what happened to us". Again tears streamed down our faces, to what use, and unashamed we rubbed our hands over our faces and took off now moved by force, departing with drooping heads. We arrived at rail tracks and what looked like an inside station, still in construction, with lots of Jewish laborers as slaves on their six month reprieve, still working or laboring away whilst barely alive ,looking at us with vacant eyes. This was still all within the camp, one can just imagine the enormous size of it all, and staggering it was like everything here. Of course selfish humans that we are, we were pleased to get away from there with the feeling of being given a hard green apple and then probably getting one less green afterwards for being such good boys, feeling on the top of the world with our temporary reprieve.

We noticed the smaller and cozier looking goods wagons in which we started entering now with S.S.'s around us in a much more jovial mood. The insides of the wagons there were, whitewashed and spread all over with disinfectant, newly made wooden latrines neatly made and painted light blue, ample rations of bread, what looked like a long and consistent loaf, lots of water and lots of room to sit and lie down.

A lanky officer jumping quickly in and out of each wagon gave us a lighthearted speech, asking if we were Arians and telling us we were going to the most organized camp in Germany, namely "Buchenwald" to work.

Our fellow comrades left behind were considered to be too sick: over two hundred where now going to get the proper and best treatment and we all knew what that implied too, of course, we would never hear of them again and they all joined the throngs in the gas and crematoriums queues very quickly, probably right now while they were talking to us. We were told they would be hospitalized, guessing our concern for them: that's something we didn't see in the camp for sure, a hospital. Soon their oils, fat and ashes would be mixed, Arian and Semite, and used for the same purposes, then to fertilization, of no difference or consequence but as a handy use for the living in unadulterated form.

We were thinking gravely now, speaking for myself and others we had never seen mass grave pits while we were there, but they were there also just like everything else we would hear about in every similar camp. The only thing they didn't have to do was to use too many bullets now to tire their arms.

Conscious or not to all that was happening, with their set minds and continuous drummed indoctrination it was like the butcher, slaughtering pigs, that was all. It had become a very ordinary daily routine and for the time being we all had to accept that, unless some force could change that.

128

There were gallows and injections but we didn't see Deither, you have got to believe that with all the rest like myself and the logical deductions one can make from the whole. If one thing is there then the other things are those to be told by the survivors.

It was mostly a variety of multiple actions and the inflicting of pain, in this superimposed hatred campaign worthy of a deep primitive background that was perpetuated with a ferocity common to the Nazis. Only humans can think that one out, mostly refined for the wrong reasons unless one takes the numbers and quantity down in a state of possibilities; but had it to be so painful and all on this certain quickness pulsated and compensated for speeds sake, the pattern plus the revenge.

Talking about numbers which very often arises in the most skeptical of circles of opposition and people of doubtful sympathies, they do not need calculators. Everybody had time now and then to monitor and enough presence of mind to calculate that five of those gas crematoriums had the capacity of killing four million people and more in three years, adding to it all the other kind of exterminations, contemplating and considering working and non-working days to the works, cleaning and overhauling etc. There was no shortage of continuous manpower in this case. Also to be considered were the other camps and the killings of before.

Four million becomes a low figure actually and an underestimation rather than an exaggeration, suddenly they seem to have forgotten the German efficiency in everything. On top of all this they were able to send work commandos to the industrial complexes, coal mines, etc, to augment their output.

After contemplation and generalizing on all of this our lanky S.S. announced the the usual rehearsed "Bon Voyage", this time as a Good Luck and we became very wary of this and now the wagons were softly closed.

Off we went onto the next voyage into the unknown. Glad to be still alive on the eleventh day since our arrival in Auschwitz.

We came and went and didn't conquer. Obviously a small change of wind had taken place concerning us. The Gestapo Bureau from Berlin had ordered that halt but still had sentenced us to die, we were going to be used as a more expert fry for some of their schemes and fervently believing in their own doctrines which they did like a new religion: they were the loyal followers of their own lies which had an inkling of first success. They had already gotten away with so much, it was all a question of absolute power and speed to overcome the unready and unprepared. This would become clear as we rolled on, with both speeds: God's speed and train speed, pushing our locomotive westward returning on this new urgency of purpose to destruction. Could the messages at home and on our journeys have contributed slightly to do with it? Let's hope so, very likely the planes had verified the existence of Auschwitz and some Nazi's themselves or other dignitaries maybe wished to let the world know something after having reached the West, maybe Jewish sections and individuals. A multiple choice of possibilities had arrived. We were on our way back to Weimar now anyway.

Relaxing in our, considered as luxury compartments, we took a bit of rest. There was no attempt at anything like escaping, it was out of the question, our brains could only absorb so much and prepare, this was like the seventh day of rest after the creation, and we rested. If you like to think about it symbolically we had crossed the Red Sea and had come out of it on the other side. This time the descendants children of Israel didn't and we were instead the multiple international crowd of a different human kind transplanted in the time cycle and the Germans, like the Egyptians, were still with us, to get their turn at the scythe they mowed with. For all of us with more to come, the crossing was far from over yet. So who will doubt that the divinity didn't play a role in all of this? Me, the least of all.

In all those human and inhuman plays, set against each other sometimes I would notice factors that seemed to be of a far superior nature than I could possibly understand, but was just about aware of.

This awareness was of some kind intelligence that worked around and in all those happenings evolving around oneself and also provided on this plane now and hereafter in a way I couldn't possibly grasp but was there somehow and could forgive but also recreated everything even better again and in an improved way above and towards an ultimate goal of serenity in itself achieving complete satisfaction and happiness in an inner contentment of being, and in joining up with what is already there foremost aiming the whole movement in development of progress to the whole.

All this provoked and resulted in the produce of a lot of energy and resolve to strive and to find by consequence solutions on an emergency basis level precipitating the whole universe ahead.

The sacrificing was and must be the result of that combustion and expansion released too profound and abruptly. Until we have a wiser and balanced viewpoint of more adjustment brought into being we have to be content to go along with it as it confronts us. So the time was made ripe for the next super-power to be brought out and actively disclose the expectations for advancement.

Of course it is all there, already provided for. So the race was in full swing now and it looked as if we were going to be part of it to, still to victory. As long as this lanky S.S. in Auschwitz gave us the "good bye" the way he did, he had done his part of the bargain and followed the orders to the hilt.

The thinning out of our ranks could be dispensed with as the weakest were no good anyway and they were replaceable, besides our status of N.N. didn't allow for any reprive anyway, we were likely to replace others, or in for a special assignment thought out by the S.S. bureau, and not for our Arian characteristics but for the way they had started their policy and their judgment accordingly to their plans, and our physiques and backgrounds.

Wondering what Buchenwald would be like, we travelled one way back to Weimar, the old republic of Saxony and Goethe's paradise or home region. The railway journey did run on time as usual and gradually we mounted the slope leading up to the wooded area of the Eisenberg, all nicely tucked away so that nobody would see too much, and guarded with everything available against intruders as well as potential escapees.

A massive cordon of the tank corps at the outer circle near the bottom of the hill looked after that part, big farms in between all warned and on the alert on the outer circle. On top of the hill a complete full S.S. training camp and then there were the actual guards with the electrical fence around the concentration camp, very congenial. It was one of the first and oldest institutions of its kind from about 1933 A.D. It started as a rehabilitation camp for dissidents in the first place and from there on got from bad to worse as time went on.

We came to a camp station just next to and outside the fence and we had the usual welcome party with ferocious dogs waiting, helping us along with the result that some of us got bitten straightaway, whole pieces of flesh were taken from our buttocks, leaving bleeding and large open wounds. This had nothing in common with the orders of the other S.S. man in Auschwitz of course and you just run for your life.

I noticed there were genuine newly built factories on my left side when I walked or rather rushed with those dogs behind me, panting and drooling for another delicious bite and onslaught on the pack. So far some true factors came to light as fact as to what he had said before our departure.

We were going to be used as a last resort for slave labor, for whatever it was, before the last judgment overtook them and in a desperate attempt at haste and speed in a last effort to win their started war. As part of the welcome society was also the obedient underdog slave drivers or camp elders and CAPO'S, from the Roman Capitano, visualizing the drummers and ramrods supervising and beating the tempo for the rowers in the galleys, and freely using the whips for their Master's sake, an ideal set-up or vast decor for a Cecil B. De Mille film that would have made.

We must have been the V.I.P's no doubt about it. Everybody had the badges of the red triangles and most of them from the guards were Germans themselves having survived the rise of the Reich with Hitler as Fuhrer and looking forward eagerly to its final fall too. They didn't consider themselves as traitors far from it, just as promotors of another policy which was like ours anyway and so they had certain rights of dignity by the Nazis left to them for not being ordinary criminals. They were mostly just a bit to the left, Communists, social democrats still called Socialists then, some Liberals and religious representatives, mostly from the Protestant inclined camps, Deserters and abnormals. They had ordinary civilian suits and berets usually of typical East European origin. The suits altered to see the markings clearly either by dye or squares sewn in with the white-blue stripes of galley prisoner, a number under the triangle on a stripped ribbon with the block and wing marks indicated, and armbands with "Capo" on them. They took charge of us instead of the S.S. beside us. The first point of interest I try to mention so, to put everybody into the picture, as it was, and our Auschwitz advertiser so nicely had put, the best camp in Germany, that was the way it looked at first glance.

132

13- Buchenwald:

The best graded in good looks to start with, built as an exemplary camp. So the first thing we saw was the crossroads, after leaving our exclusive station location behind us. Four roads crossing similar to the kind used in the woods. Even Walt Disney could have made something wonderful out of it, but for grown-ups only.

That's it "Buchenwald", struck one as a wonderland in reverse, it couldn't have been bettered. Hans Anderson could have been at work here. I remember all the details clearly which is all important for now, as well as for what would happen later in the days of the expiring throes of the fiery dragon's last coiling in agony of death trying to crush the nearest to him with it. Auschwitz looked more like a forest with death trees sticking out of the bog, very bare in comparison with this camp, which in contrast had the superb view of a glorified holiday resort.

In the center of the four crossroads, exactly where they met, was a small dark green grass patch elevation and a pole very much like a totem pole with four planks pointed at the ends as ideal road indicators or sign posts. On those planks and clearly drawn and painted in caricature style showing in one direction the proud S.S. marching as figures in full regalia with weapons also in the number of fours.
This was towards their quarters, which were high rising flats of a somber grey color sticking up in the distance.

The other four, the inmates-prisoners as we were made to be, foremost and first an affluent Jewish capitalist dispatched with the yellow star of King David on him, then a political prisoner with the red triangle, then a criminal with the green triangle and last a purple, black and blue triangle representing all the others, which alternatively in combination represented religion, homosexuals, saboteurs and deserters.

The fourth road was "Gouzloff Werke", those factory installations next to the station with the thick woods at the other side of the tracks.

Gouzloff, a German capitalist or rather industrialist and main shareholder of the company situated on the eastern side of Germany was like Krupp's Werkes, ordered by the Gestapo bureau to fulfill their patriotic commitment and to build factories for their sole use around this camp's installations, particularly to employ the Politickers, that was us, as slave labor. We were their property now, body and soul to do what they liked with us, nobody else, no free workers, nor forced labor or anybody of any kind would come in for this exclusive treatment. Our files went with us and we still would be executed accordingly when the time came.

When such was demanded near or at the best disposal times and squads discretion or on direct orders from Berlin our executions would be carried out. Our deaths could also come about in the meantime by hard labor in the quarry or strassen-bau or road construction, bomb disposal squad, starvation, diseases, beatings, firing squad by machine guns, hangings, injections, torture and chopping off of heads: if necessary that was the privilege of another department outside, you were sent for: There were a few refinements on demand and applications by the S.S. butchers and S.S. doctors of the institute for garroting with piano wires or meat hooks, dissecting, medicinal experiments and even space technology, atmospheric pressure, etc, to be applied. The human guinea pigs where there and in ample supply and available at any time. According to this we had reached the top of the summit of all ambitions.

There was a tower too, the Bismarck Tower, faintly I could see the silhouette in the mist and under it where the broken bodies of so many buried in mass graves. An ugly reminder for such a glorious war memorial and what it stood for has never been seen since, but if Bismarck could have looked down from this place he might have been pleased with the continuity of his overdisciplined Germany and its offspring.

Beyond the workplaces towards Weimar, near to a double gate with more fences, was the treehouse of Goethe himself in which he wrote many of his best works and relaxed there, that part we couldn't see from where we walked now, but one indicator also pointed to Weimar just the same.

The road of the prisoners and the camp so nicely captioned was called "Caracho Weg" in Russian and meaning the Good road or paradise way, so Buchenwald might as well have been called Shangri-La too. The sarcasm of it all had just begun.

We were just about to reach two guard houses on each side of the road with two representatives of this mock paradise ordering "Mutzen ab" caps off pointing their weapons at us.

134

An enormous eagle perched on a pillar was set in the middle carved in stone hewn from the quarry. On a wooden board above the guardhouse entrances was inscribed in Gothic script: "Recht oder Unrecht mein Vaterland" Right or Wrong my country. I don't know whether this excuse was more for them than us, but to commit wrongness in the name of patriotism was certainly wrong. It brings to mind the saying "Patriotism is the last refuge of a scoundrel". Once this epitome of events passed we came to the habitat of the Commandant "half way house", well-constructed on the left of us with a garden and two soixante-quinze guns in front of it, a reminder of the 1914 -1918 war, retaken in 1940. You could call him a son of a gun then. The house was in the Caracho way and quite nice. No formal greetings here that would be coming. On our right we could see the electrical fence and some of the camp site sloping downwards and a lane of trees for coverage between us.

The setting and decor was still ideal and grand, it would get better, further. As we proceeded, we walked as if to eternity from one surprise to another. Continually going ahead towards the sunset now or in the morning to the sunrise, heads bobbing up and down.

We came to what looked like part of an actual zoo, dropped in from some endangered area to lighten our burden or impress potential visitors mostly. Indeed as it was they came from the Berlin Tiergarden Zoo, put in a safe place away from the regular bombing, there and under the protection of the camp and us like the Gouzloff-Werke, where better.

There was of course the rock garden with Baboons showing their usual bald bottoms to us and there was also a black bear present and we guessed right, better fed than we would be, too.

Behind them was a dug out space with a ramp of soil to receive the impact of the machinegun bullets from the ripped in half victims placed on the wooden stakes, more often to be replaced than not. I suppose the barking of the dog baboons assisted in muffling up the noise they made.

One can comprehend how the nerves of the animals became agitated with moments like that, every time there were executions carried out. From now on we could wait in our dimmed views, the big center tower looking over the camp above the gate with a short curve to the right, having cellular constructions extending from the base, those were the execution or torture cells on each side of this control tower, or for the quick interrogations and also for the firing squad days and guillotine transports!!! When you entered or marched out one step, which was being closely watched, and the "Mutzen ab" order, again then you had the privilege to hear the best band in Germany performing for your benefit, or beating time, dressed in the most colorful uniforms taken from a nineteenth century orchestra or military capelle, looking like real clowns or a circus band. These people, by the way, where the musicians of the Philharmonic Orchestra of Prague, taken as hostages for some disturbances in Czechoslovakia at the time. Only the best was good enough with this.

Around the camp there where the many "Miradors" as the French called them, or watchtowers manned by a machine gunner with search light and two more soldiers. On the center tower there where several searchlights, placed on the balcony from where the administration could watch the crowds to be counted and the entity of the whole camp as it was on a slope in the shape of a nearly perfect pentagon.

On a clear day we could see the statue of Barbarossa which was an enormous obelisk in the distance. The Swedish Field Marshall and conqueror of renown.

More often than not, in the late season we were covered with a mist or rather low passing clouds. Turning in from the corner end our band stood, the Commandant in the company of his wife named Ilse Koch, of a certain fame, and his S.S. Handlangers were there. Whips ready, we would be faced with the gate in wrought iron and on the bars in letters about the height and width of a man. "Yedem dad Seine" "To Each his Own".

That would be like the entrance of hell on the way to heaven, guarded by a devil and his demons. Only Saint Peter was absent. The gates opened for us and we would enter now. The grand scene was like stepping into a picture display laid on in front us in unsurpassed grandeur, a great spectacle of pitiful confinement so gorgeous under this lower sky with the restricted feeling and wishing that one could fly away forever on the wings of imagination to freedom. The music still kept droning on driving us on to jail. It was very beautiful in its ugliness and gave one the feeling of reaching to the heights of Golgotha and you could also be crucified here, right now, on the altar of a despotism the like of which the world had never before seen. It was impressive and overwhelming, well done. A big open place reached the first confines of the wooden billeting's, followed row by row of two story stone buildings and then proceeding approximately one mile or more long. Below that more buildings, from a real brothel to an indoctrination hall for propaganda films and picture taking, no lectures. In between, the junior camp as the lower camp was called, and the senior camp a quarantine camp with two or four rows in depth again and just as long. On your left was a small first aid or hospital, to your right was the crematorium indistinguishable, sticking out just the same, but no gas-chambers, which we were used to now.

Smaller in size than a single building in Auschwitz, similar to the last one we saw with the little boys. Then the entering and shaving blocks again with a change of clothing going on and finally the large kitchen. The kitchen building struck us as not very big for the camp size. The hanging tree of Goethe was in front of it all and center with the concrete trenches still present to dangle in the victims after being pushed, it was coming into bloom now and was a big thick oak, where Goethe used to sit writing and looking at the landscape beyond as we had just done on entering, he very likely in serene meditation not realizing what would come after his passing away in the century before this one.

His own compatriots would put their signatures in their own blood on the place where he sat, clearing it from bush and trees, removing the rocks and building everything that was there today.
We would be the next residents after they were murdered and then it would be our turn.

Hitting the bucket, was a common expression for worse periods of deprivation and our planned expiry time, there was alleviation in between. Sometimes we went through such pauses otherwise no living souls would have survived it, very much similar to during the flood, the severity of the punishment. There had to be a salvation for all the international crowds as represented here to be able to float upon the waters of the atrocities and survive it.

Talking about dry land, there was a strip of used land left in the lower corner and some green vegetables grown. For the kitchen, maybe for the S.S., senior German prisoners tended it and must have had the benefits of it. The Ark eventually on dry land was the invisible underground resistance movement that was able to evolve out of this international melee inside the sphere of such horror. Buchenwald would carry inside her belly a child that would within the protection of the womb would be born and come into existence, and produce an effect of the greatest magnitude for its own cause. If we had to perish this was our total revenge.

Driven and entering the sorting and shearing rooms again, we had enough time to pick further information up made available by the senior prisoners given so gullibly to us.

It was now the 14th of May, 1944 and we were facing a new period of detention with a diminished group but the majority still present so far. The CAPOs and the helpers guiding us and telling all under the surveillance of a single S.S., and warning us about good behavior all the time, mostly for obeying the orders promptly. At all times to be subservient and at the will of our masters, right or wrong to the extreme of what one could bear, be unobtrusive.

It was also better for one not to be decorated in beautiful tattoo's, they told us, keep the fellow out of view if you have any among you, because the wife of the Commandant had a peculiar hobby and picked those out for the covering of lampshades. This was Ilse Koch spying from secret holes and compartments, at the potential candidates and anything else unemployment that appealed to her morbid satisfaction.

We were shaved again allover our bodies and bathed too. Our clothes of Auschwitz were exchanged for striped ones and the red triangles with numbers of this camp. The cruel stories that came to our ears, where an unending nightmare and a reminder that we were still involved.

There was also a bureau to sort us out for the best use for our labor. Behind the S.S. buildings there was a quarry supplying all the stones for the camp and roads and even contracts for further afield. In between there were more animals in a place called "Valkenhof" falcon house, to a fenced park shelter for deer and boar to be kept and tended by us. There were Villas for the V.I.P.'s.

Since 1944 to 1945 the extent of the camp made the close contact with the different 'einsatz-groups' of the S.S., less possible to have an individual base of concentration, at this time.

The resistance was also getting stronger and better organized than ever among the best of the international partisans gathered there.

We arrived at the right time to join up. This had been started by the German inmates themselves long ago, of which eighty per cent had disappeared by now. There were personalities still present like Richard Thalmann, Hood, and Walter Poller himself released before we came in 1940. From our side there was Blum being the Brussels redactor of the newspaper Le Peuple, a DeWever dentist from Antwerp and so many other representatives of diverse politics not just the left.

These committees were formed from all political opinions and not like the press and not her envious chauvinistic sources would like to infer and thus nullify our combined efforts.

The National Committees formed an International Resistance one which justified the survival of the fittest besides giving aid to all others in the measures and climate of a clandestine action, created in the utmost secrecy and use of counter-infiltration with some of the enemy itself. The above names mentioned only constitute a few of all the Social Democrats, Socialists, Communists Liberals and Progressive Conservatives from all the national sections amongst us and others.

Everybody was there, present inside continuing the anit-Nazi battle as much as on the outside; maybe even a bit more, considering our imprisonment. Rivalry and Chauvinism would also raise its head up traditionally and the question of bias and small mindedness was always rife and present, to our dismay and the Nazi's merriment. This was practically unavoidable and would hamper our desperate efforts to the opposite, so much sometimes as to take credit away from our sincere endeavors, which I say here as a real disservice to our honor and credit of the highest order being dragged in the mud by this vile slurring.

After all these new confrontations we moved slowly to the lower camp1a quarantine camp. There we could verify most of the things we heard. Here we were back in an Auschwitz atmosphere and dirty still quagmire with closed barracks, one blanket, open pit toilets and outside washing pipes with troughs. This place was separated from the upper or senior camp by a fence again and from the brothel and indoctrination hall below us, too.

Apart from the separation and controls for three weeks we received so many injections that we were warned to try and dodge them by passing them through the skin pressed between our fingers, inside one way and out the other if possible. As it was done by the camp helpers, under a Capo and S.S. who couldn't always be everywhere this was the method to employ while he was distracted.

During the quiet spells we searched for lost friends and at other transports for news and acquaintances from home.

We were also taken to the indoctrination block to be photographed, measured and receive new numbers. Then we were shown an S.S. film about their superior qualities in training and fighting which we had to watch. Nothing about cruelty, as they had enough experience of that with the prisoners in the camp and for us to look at. After that our new numbers were sewn on the coats and trousers which were stripped.

We explored a bit further our new place of confinement. There was also some camp money in circulation, marks that could be changed. We would receive that for our first work commando which was the quarry for sure, a touch of the hardest slave labor to begin with.

The quarry was called "Steinbuck" and was oh the southern side of the hill looking upon the forested undulations of Franconia and Bavaria, the nearest town being Eisenach. This would be an ideal point for getting away if it was not for a very close chain of guards towards the open window views. When misty or low clouds were about they doubled the guard. The grey uniforms Totenkaphen with four black foreign S.S. entwining Ukrainians. They had formed their international too, in the style of the Nazi's of course.

On one of our off duty days we followed a black marketer who convinced us how to get rid of our money and led us to the rear at the other end of the quarantine camp where we met two poor desolated figures huddled together in a corner, still in fairly good condition, so that's what the money exchange was for, for those miserable still speculating. One turned out to be grandfather Michelin and the other an Armenian millionaire who sold crucifixes and other paraphernalia at Lourdes before having received their wages for sin here. This practice of course was looked at with distaste by the other prisoners, they had their spies and ferrets too, in the camp who informed them about this.

In no time our black marketer was spotted and chased and we warned not to take any heed of him.

140

On the way back we noticed a prisoner with two buckets full of stones and sand standing fixed on a wooden box.

This one had stolen food from his comrades, realizing what severe punishment they would hand out if caught we quickly took the lesson.

This camp was also like an underworld, full of petty intrigue and corruption. After a while in quarantine all pent up revenge on suspected and guilty traitors would break loose and a quick trial was executed. This would be done by sharp instruments brought in by the commandos, drowning by holding the heads down in the troughs surrounded by the crowd, or chasing a fellow out in the evening at curfew with no other alternative than throwing themselves on to the barbed wire near the electrical fence to be shot simultaneously from the "Miradors". They were not always suicides as shown in photos. The S.S. didn't care a bit and the bodies, were just added to the rest laying along the block with the others to be taken away by the "leich tragers", body carriers, to the crematorium, with its yard infested by rats and other vermin, the mouths of the victims open and limbs broken before burning and thrown on a death pile until ready for cremation.

The Jews in Buchenwald had almost completely disappeared, either to Auschwitz, Bergen-Belsen or Mathausen. There were thirty still amongst us, strong builders and probably more that I didn't know about, the rest were mixed with us and un- known to anybody. We saw the shoe piles left, from the past, only the uppers, the soles had been used by other prisoners.
Camps independent from Buchenwald would be filled such as Dora, Laura and the terrible SII near Ohringen where gigantic factories were constructed unknown to the outside world.

Personal fights in desperation amongst us only landed people up in the crematorium. The people killed as traitors, which I was able to witness, were guilty without a doubt as far as I could make out.

On our trip we had indifferently watched an individual from Eastern Europe flattering the S.S. around us in a very obvious manner. French inmates kept him in mind and knew he had given them away in the jails of France on several occasions: despised by his mates he was likewise by the Germans for it, they loathed him, his ways and manners gave him the look of a creep. One day his ordeal came to pass, he was stabbed in the side with a small sharp needle, smuggled in from the Guzloff-Werke, several times and gradually driven to the trough and there pushed in and held under water till drowned.

I remember his accusers, looking around for others after that straightaway, it was too easy once done, such was the mood, and people were apt to commit bestialities with impunity and no second thoughts about it.

One of the Capos had become as crude and cruel as the S.S. themselves, he would beat prisoners up in the most cruel way with his stick until they were falling and lying flat on the ground and then kicked them to the delight of the watching S.S. This one had to go to for sure, one way or the other.

The food was deficient in nourishment and our hard labor in the quarry extremely heavy. This was another weeding out process for the toughest. There was no respite: the round the clock S.S. bullies were on our backs all the time, the whips wound around their wrists ready for the first one they could catch, especially if one was trying to hide in the crevices. We could act a bit luckily, the pick going up and down breaking next to nothing, the only way to survive and last the days out a bit longer. Sometimes we were put from six to a dozen in number in the harness, a stick placed across the chest to pull the slabs up the slope of the quarry.

One day I dropped just down at noonday and fell in the only patch of clover I could ever have seen in the place, picking up a four leafed clover which I kept for a very long time in a small religious book with my diary meticulously written on a couple of pages, it came out with me too.

My ankle got knocked and wounded when I slipped among the cliffs and rocks one day. The old prisoners told us those stones were poisonous and to make sure we didn't get scratched. It never healed properly but I managed as I had to and never to give up but to persevere at all times, through thick and thin. The fleas and lice in the block were a terrible nuisance. I had big holes on the same leg as the wounded ankle and it gave me trouble where I had been bitten too at the same time. One could put his little finger in some of them; it looked like beriberi not enough nourishment lacking vitamin C to assist the healing process. If a flea bite could do that much harm you could imagine how the other wounds fared.

The people bitten by the dogs when we arrived died in agony shortly afterwards, mostly by tetanus•. People still kept dying and transports where in the offing again. I stayed on and I do not know why. Puzzle. Eventually I passed the labor exchange and was consigned to Gouzloff Werke and to the Upper Camp or rather Senior Camp now, the luck of the draw or maybe picked, I don't know. After the stripes another suit with squares on instead of indelible dye, it seemed I was chosen. My haircut was pretty normal too, not in the Iroquois style of cocks comb.

I had a cross interrogation by the elders of my block too, what seemed like a very expert and well trained agent in such matters, he was Belgian and came from somewhere near Poperinge and had been in Moscow and belonged to a Belgian resistance group, in other words he was a communist agent and commissar, another foreign powers intelligence too. He was chosen for the job because he could verify many of my regions, recognition points and my immediate background in Ostend, my place of origin. They already knew some of my exploits through other prisoners, like my escape, reliability and knowledge.

It seemed that I fitted into their organization and pattern of operations, having contacts on the outside was very important.

I was in their hands and I am convinced also in other peoples too. I didn't know very well yet but all involved. I was channeled mostly unaware but observed well in different commandos where escapes were most likely and possible extra food supplies became easier. They never told me to do so, it was completely up to me. My outfit was also provided in preparation, on the other hand if I had been caught just for that I was in for it, but I had the luck of innocence with me. Further as an escapee, once already, and re-captured, I never had an exclusive striped suit with big targets on it like other escapees were forced to wear, and only in special harsh commando's put as soon they arrived, always guarded by dog• patrols and S.S. at the ready. I don't know who I had to thank for that but it was as if my- file had been changed or disappeared, of course the organization was looking after me if my file had gone.

I was still there, so danger was lurking in all quarters, we weren't invisible to that extent but it helped insomuch. We because, although numbers of death could be changed and so forth, the lazy S.S. if need be could nose further than that by suspicion and sometimes they did. The confusion was helped along with so much going on that it was even too much for this German over efficiency. Sometimes we thought they played with darts to pick some victims eventually, but you still heard them over the loud speakers and as always we sat in fear one minute after the other expecting to hear our name or number being called. We never saw anybody coming back from those calls. Often the S.S. had to come and fetch their victims and drive them up like reluctant animals to the slaughter, realizing very well that their time was up.

I can see all these episodes vividly in my mind as clearly as the day they happened. We just slithered throughout it by sheer luck, resilience, strength and endurance. You had to be like a Samson for your own sake also very much like a soldier at the front, there was really not much difference except he could shoot at the enemy, we may too if and when a weapon would be provided.

There was no way you could join the S.S. either however desperate they became and towards the end their numbers were dwindling although a lot where of mixed natures and origins now and the standards going down with their categories. What did occur was a fact that you could join the army of the damned, under the impression that you could make a quick getaway. That was something that we had it not thought about as far as I know. A few German homosexuals tried it out to be destroyed in the process, you can imagine, that's where they put them in between them and the Russians.

I don't know where one's breaking point was that's "To Each His Own" that differed greatly: some people have never talked and given anybody away, others did under the simplest or the most refined tortures.

My block was now next to the fence, in the Guinea Pig block or experimental block. It was also the center of the combined operations of the resistance, we were the main group. The network was spread out in all the other blocks evenly. The biggest threat were the German Greens, they were the scoundrels and rascals, also still patriots and used as ferrets, Bo we had to replace and get rid of them by concessions given to us by the S.S. due to our status.
As they needed us to fulfill their programs of new weapons for delivery we had to be accounted for more and more and our rights as political prisoners was considered and first in line with the way the war was now going.

This was achieved eventually for the biggest part of it with a transition that sent the worst elements into oblivion. Sometimes we were supplied with a bit more food from this point of consideration for a very short time too. A thin porridge in the morning and Austrian cigarettes supplied for the S.S. not for long and it was back to Magorka, consisting of chopped up stems of Russian tobacco plants, also once only the bottom of the dregs of the country's vineyards from the Moselle where given to us and could be bought with our Marks, something to buy for and all those small pauses gave us a breather.

By June or July the heat was pretty constant so our small slice of bread with a finger of margarine was supplied the evening before during the watery soup round with sometimes the addition of a small amount of salami or jam. This was all experimental stuff or most of it, figured out to see how far we could go, just on this economic survival rationing and still be of use to them.

The bread consisted of a lot of potato flour with straw in it and other local products with only some of the wheat present as far as we knew, mostly chestnuts and birch nuts flour for the remainder. The margarine and jam where all concoctions and produce from the coal industry. The meat or salami, unknown to us in its countenance was about one half of an inch thick and one inch wide, didn't last out either in its meagre supply. If you wonder whether cannibalism had taken place, yes we had all heard of it, in quarantine from incoming transports. Sometimes the rations were made smaller to suit the effect and then the ravages were terrible after it. One day a body laying outside to be collected in the morning was missing a foot. Nobody saw it and it happened in quarantine with new arrivals coming from worse conditions, coming over to die anyway which was more constant than usual near the end.

We know today that the rocks of Steinbruck quarry are a high grade of concentrated active uranium ore: that's why they were observed to be of a poisonous content by the old prisoners. The Germans possessed the stuff in their own back yard unbeknown to them, a real surprise that was. The Russians made a catching up use of the rich uranium, as it was plentiful, in their militarized zone after the Potsdam Conference and the Yalta agreement of dividing the two Germanys up.

It probably wouldn't have made a great difference because the race for the heavy water from Norway would have been a quickening up process with the enriched uranium and they must have had some, but in the long term it would have been to their advantage depending on how successful they would have been left alone to develop this procedure in all haste.

To begin with, the British with Norwegian Commando's succeeded if not to blow up the Hajanger project to begin with, at least to slow down predominantly and destroy the first batch of drums in the harbor.
As I saw my time out in Steinbruck in August 1944, I was assigned to Middle or Mi-bau, the Eastern part of the center buildings still under construction for Gouzloff; there were trenches to be made for strong thick cables, roads and smaller annexes to be finished off.

The road works were called 'Entwalterung'. All this was done under the close scrutiny and control of a patrolling S.S. and nearest to the last guard fence of the works with the gate end towards Weimar, also by Ukrainian S.S. black-shirts, supplemented and watched. Somehow they would try to socialize with us and share the small cobs of sweet corn which were the results of the latest experiments made by German food specialists.

This fraternization was becoming dangerously close to a catastrophe for all of us as there was a particular S.S. continually sneaking up on us to catch somebody, the prisoners by preference, to obtain his three day vacation bonus, in finding reasons for a victim to punish taken for some form of disobedience.

We were getting overconfident in using our hiding place to eat the rations saved in between to absolve our hunger pangs. Somehow we may also have been given away and on a signal he might have been informed, a victim was ready in the trap, by the black-shirts. So it happened, when my turn came and I tasted and tried that coal tar jam suddenly bees appeared from nowhere, I had never seen or noticed any before in that place, to prove that the coal tar was still good after millions of years for consumption by humans also with them, and just as surprising to me the bad product of the S.S. popped up in the unfinished doorway giving a grin of grim satisfaction his sadistic nature being worked up to a peak. I hardened myself for what was to come but knew also that I had to contain my violent strength to be used as a last resort at the end if I had to, similar to before.

Slowly he came to stand in front of me his legs wide apart studying my badges and putting his gloves on in the meantime. He had another strange close look at my red triangle with nationality and was ready now, so was I. Then he told me to stand straight to attention and not to move, all in strict orders. With his full strength and weight behind it he swung his fist in a right hook and told me to stand to attention again giving a left punch now, on both occasions right on the jaws, I went halfway down on every swing but straightened up again for the next.

He knew I was tough and hard and I saw amazement in his eyes now, more an admiration than a further challenge, probably he was hurt too and tired out. As a last resort he picked up a plank of arm's length size about two by one inches thick laying nearby and grinned again in self-gratification of the relief for him. Facing me full frontal again he indicated to the entrance opening for the door and told me to make a run for it as soon as he gave the order. I had to by-pass him of course, which he carefully obstructed and would make my run more difficult to avoid the bumping. His game was worse than Cat and Mouse play as all the dice were on his side, but I persevered. There was no choice but to endure what I was about to receive. So I started on my way at his yelling without bumping into him with the awful result of my ducking to the right I got the full impact of the sway of the stick in the center of my back.

By now my sense of feeling had gone numb, as on previous occasions during my escapes and also my state of being as hard as the stick itself, now. So the instrument of torture snapped without throwing it at all, unknown to him and without breaking or going numb. When he applied the following six beats in all seven, they came to be only half as hard as the first one. He was astonished and amazed, told me to get on with my job in the trench taking a last look at me.

I lifted the pick up as if nothing had happened and worked strenuously as if nothing had happened, and that, until he was very well out of sight and then suddenly the reactions were setting in and I could feel the pain in my jaws and could hardly move them after a while, my back was not too bad.

A boiling anger for revenge was the next thing that swelled up in me. I never met up with him again until he was killed at the liberation time. For myself I came to the conclusion that if I had to I could probably walk through a wall with toughening up. The sores gave me trouble for a couple of days more and also taught me not to trust anybody not even for a few seconds and was the best alternative I could take. Often in the dawn of morning, waiting our turn to go out of the gate, marching and moving up and down with our solemn heads facing the sunrise now we were watched all the time by the angels of death for the slightest mistake with the music   driving us by might of force.

I wondered about the first Commandos, the ones guarded by dogs, with grotesque big targets displayed on them, they were always diminishing in number every day; the escapees, I could have been one of them by now. I had to keep silent not talk to others and accept my position not wondering too much.

The Russian prisoners, some were soldiers, others suspected commissars, with their drab green uniforms and pointed hats like Mongolian and Tartar Huns bobbing up and down steadily leading the long column ahead of us marching in rhythm, passing the Caracho Weg, the guards, the eagle and away.
On one command of the eternal Mutzen ab, or a poke of the bayonet or even worse to happen we were like robots moving silently along hardly aware of the fading music in the distance played by frozen fingers in the same rhythm, the woods and trees weeping with crystal dew drops all in array of another nice morning, not for us deep in thought. The baboons and bear must have been still asleep, too cold for them. What was the use of watching the suffering of boring mankind?

A short while after this daily performance I landed up in Gouzloffwerke: my trade school background had helped with the assistance of the underground movement.

We were by now well acquainted with Gouzloff-Werke but it was still a big and great unknown even for us.

It was from those auspicious elements in society that we had been given the different placement and for a short time earned the extra porridge and were supplied with some dregs of wine and cigarettes, although the work was easier and more refined than hard labor in the quary that's the way of the world or rather as the cookie crumbles. The Ukrainians could smoke their Magorka with newspapers thrown away by the S.S. it was like flaming torches in big clouds of bellowing smoke.

My first placement was also the first department of the workshop, an assembly of small electrical components on benches with drilling of bakelite flat panel, fitting both together afterwards with a terminal hole for antenna in the middle. A guide system certainly, for what? There were also milling and drilling Machines spread out. One Civil Engineer

148

and two female assistants as silent partners, the first ones we had seen in a long time, a renewed experience. Some seniors, they showed us the ropes and intricacies of the job.

I managed a convivial short chat standing back with the technician, the woman kept well away from us. The technician was rather casual and jovial talking about Ostend which he knew very well, before the war, and had enjoyed the resort it was then, he said. We had to stop the conversation as Tom Mix came along on patrol, that was an older S.S. watching what we were all doing, like being good boys now.

He noticed numbers on our arms from Auschwitz and was curious how we landed here and felt rather uneasy about it, how the upper command had let us out I suppose. It was unheard of before our enchanted trip. Everybody watched closely until he was out of sight. The first thing that surprised me was the senior, a Frenchman under the supervisor's watchful eyes cracking all the black panels in front of him and throwing most of them away, after pushing the drills down hard and telling me so to do. If that was the play I was game of course without having any idea of being shot for it on the spot, somehow it seemed alright. The sabotage was on, in full swing now.

All the panels that passed had almost invisible cracks like that, those too bad were just thrown away for scrap. Offhand he would tell me to be a bit more careful, that's all. The civilian that is, so he knew the score. Those panels were guides to something, but what? Was it for submarines, planes or a new system altogether. It was a closed secret and being a closed shop for us too, newcomers to it all but it would make us think, nevertheless. That lot seemed to be in it alright, here, right over their heads by the looks and so were with it.

The civilian looked like a clever man to me more like the modern scientists for the space age, a Werner VonBraun type, tall blond, thin and full of intense energy, on the other hand he could have been the arch type of the ideal S.S. man they portrayed on their typical Germanic Aryan specimens they so much desired to visualize or rather back breed.

Anyway he managed to put me in a complete state of awareness to what in the hell was going on and as he was the boss I had to accept it and logically be the forced victim or the willing innocent bystander, like a lamb.

Sundays we had off and I was busy walking around in the morning to the wooden barracks near the appeal or gathering place which we were allowed to do, eagerly looking for recognizable faces. That was one of the first rounds I had dared trying always not to be too obvious and stay in the background. Again I met Janek as always I should say. Here the prophecy came to its own now and to our realization and knowledge of the tragic prediction at the table in Fort Du-Ha about meeting on a hill. He was well established with the Polish patriots in his block and already knew the score of the underground activities. He knew more than I did anyway by the sound of it. He didn't tell very much except about the thing in Guzloff. It was definitely a secret project and weapon and therefore most likely, a top secret weapon, much more than anything else.

Our next meeting would bring us closer together still and see whether we could help each other, he had to go now. My bringing into line for courier preparation was probable, taking the upper hand and I had to be told everything anyway, by my own section in the block I was in.

There was a more mature indentured courier launched well before me: I was put on the reserve, in case of his failure, only then would I be activated for sure. My full acknowledgement until the appropriate time was not all that much desired in case of complications. It takes time to be a full-fledged anything. In the meantime I noticed that just next to where I got my square bashing that they did the delicate job of rifle pointing, the prisoners themselves in charge.

Eventually a combined delegation of Red Cross and who knows what appeared and was allowed to look at Buchenwald so said which proved that the news had leaked out alright and that our courier had reached the target. The Resistance already knew the good news and also coded messages had been deciphered from the radio, on which a look and search raid was mounted on the camp by the S.S. now. They never found anything to go on, little did they know that treason in their own ranks was an accomplished fact to our full advantage.

The delegation's visit happened to be perfectly timed with the air alarms present so that we would be going out in the woods for protection against aerial bombardment, among the tall pines easily visible from the air and altitude they would be flying on the day. All for easy recognition from the air and reconnaissance of our positions below in co-ordination with each other. This was well organized on a grand scale because the target was of all importance too.

150

Our exercise was kept up like this till this memorial day of the twenty third of August, 1944, well after they left. The pressure had been continuously kept on all the time so that they wouldn't give them any relaxation in case they kept us again in Gouzloff werke inside.

On this lovely day then I was just nicely and lazily settling under a nice thick tree looking at the foliage on top of me and the very clear sky, when we heard the familiar droning of the planes coming on, but this was suddenly quite different, it increased very much so at a lower altitude now to the attacking speed and the full preparation which I straight away recognized as it, full speed go, let all loose.

They came steadily in close formation like a holocaust of their own judgment, assuming deadly ghostly appearance. The first wave similar to whitish speedy crosses, with the bouncing sunlight rays on their coffins, like bodies and dangerously just visible in the openings amongst the foliage above us, and causing me to quickly flatten myself beneath the tree I had just been sitting against. I only could see the amazement and whitish staring fear in the friend's eyes facing me, and still sitting on his haunches, looking upwards to the sky. In no time he was flat next to me and practically on top of me, the only place left.

Now we heard the mass of big destructive bombs coming down incessantly, screeching. It was as if the air above us was torn open, there was hissing not so much whistling altogether at once, loud and heavy it came as the impact exploded around us, most of the noise was heard better far away from us as we were laying lower to it than anything alive, but the air wall moved among and mostly above us pressing everything further away down and pushing on like a wind of hurricane force. Making me press myself as flat against the ground as I possibly could, I felt myself being lifted up and down like a feather and I had just put a twig into my mouth to save my eardrums from the blasts, an old soldiers trick.

There were terrible screams coming from all over as a couple of bombs had dropped just near the entrance of the forest. More and more people piled on top of me for protection now as if in a safe haven. A lot of dust whirled up and obscured the sunlight but more planes were still coming on and suddenly long shining sticks were dropping among us impaling quite a few of the unfortunate prisoners on the forest floor and instantly exploding all over the place, that's how thickly they covered the forest floor for every one man's length.

Some of us started running wildly only to be splattered by the immense fire bits from exploding incendiary bombs, those were the objects we were being hit with by now, those infernal things being so light got blown or rather sucked backwards towards a vacuum created by the former explosions and by a counter wind that blew them off target. Besides dust there was also smoke and fire and more cries of victims all intermingled like Hell Fire. Also the rush was on as the guardian S.S. had retreated down the slope a bit more and in the bushes ready for the onslaught that would come towards that direction which I could see to be working up too. Better to stay put, this was no time for a mass breakout unless we had been prepared for it and had known it would happen like this, but even the pilots did not envisage this turn of events.

It wasn't long before as I was pondering and watching that I heard the short bursts of machine gun fire, rifles and pistol salvos resounding from the direction of the massive rush and more screams again. The rest of the crowd coming running back towards us now, they got no further than that. The S.S. following on their heels, luckily with the shooting stopping, saying to us that's what your friends did to you and all, pointing to the victims in agony and other deaths. All of us looking in awe and disbelief at friends with their intestines hanging out of their bellies, which were ripped open
.
This was the fruits of war and the accidents with it, nobody knew which the worst was, but one provoked the other. There was no safe course in between the battling opposites. The poor fellows that were trapped had run from the frying pan into the fire, from being torn to pieces one minute to the piercing bullets in the other minute. I don't know of any battle that is worse or better, it is, all "To Each His Own" over and over again.

The theme would return till it was over and done with. The ultimate price we all had to pay friend and foe alike with the relentless march of the conquerors and their war horses.

I noticed the S.S. was not brandishing their pistols so much when one of them said that he was just as much in a state of shock as us, which was good to serve on them. He let us walk back, unmolested to pick up our wounded, who cared about the dead at this instant, nobody.

One of my unfortunate friends was completely disembodied and we felt like he was putting his entrails   back, but far beyond the point of pain and just smiled peacefully at us, still having presence of mind. He expired quickly after that, with us both holding hands. He was the one that told us about keeping a stick or twig in our mouths during the impact of explosions. Holding and supporting a couple shot in the leg we came to an open clearing near the entrance of the forest, by avoiding the big gaping craters and looking on the left side back to the Guzloff-Werke there was nothing remaining as far as we could see, a few walls and ruins with pits. Total destruction had been achieved beyond that nothing, a few walls here and there breaking the view, a grandiose view of almost complete devastation. That was only a quick glance because we hurried to get back into the camp, struggling with the wounded hopping in between us.

An eerie and dusty atmosphere prevailed over all and was trying to settle back. Souls departed after the destruction but their sacrifice had not been in vain. A peculiar rushing noise was heard over the scene like over the battle of Waterloo or just the wind with our own pent up imagination.

I observed the high rise S.S. buildings were untouched. For a moment disappointment overwhelmed us about the injustice of it, but not for long, as we saw all their shelters destroyed without exception in front of it completely ploughed over like a harvester had cleared the land in preparation before the sowing, but at the same time had destroyed all the vermin sheltering within.

The S.S. from the buildings and around had all run as one man into those quick covered gangways and mazes from the shrapnel and the waves of judgment rolling overhead had been made to release all their heavy loads from Guzloff towards the buildings, to fulfillment of their wrath in this deadly carpet bombing so that the main stream had come exactly down in the right area. There must have been a good bit of planning and precision put into this, the rest was the Lord's. Only the best pilots were good enough for this kind of operation.

The S.S. who were in training were killed en masse in what I say they would have liked to inflict upon us and our people. Justice after all had taken place on a grand scale of retribution. The carnage among them must have been tenfold to ours if not more likely, we will never know the exact figures, but it was satisfying to know the score was being evened out.

153

Their bodies wouldn't be burned with ours, the others would stay buried where they became entombed, too much trouble to unearth them and to do the same somewhere else.

The remarkable outstanding occurrences noticed in this holocaust of right and wrong for my country, were the small flames, licking from the same beams with the slogans in Gothic, crawling upwards snake wise like the finality of that saying. The Guards weren't there, we never looked for them, and they were probably in the shelters too, only twenty yards away and couldn't be found.

No "Mutzen ab" no hats off, now "Versekwunden". The top heavy eagle had been taken up and blown fifty yards away laying on its side as if hit by a giant. The totem pole was in a hundred splinters with a "voltreffer" right landed on its side. To my total amazement most of the prisoners were still walking. So as we were caring for our wounded, transporting them in batches, sorrowful and amazed at it all but still more intact and with a new glow of hope burning inside us, we pulled ourselves together quicker than the S.S . We had our heads raised and didn't see one S.S. for a while, it was like the earth had swallowed them up, which it really had done, with only the worms having a laid out feast on their rotting cadavers.

Contrary to their sarcastic poem and inscription above the crematorium for us intended:

Nicht onhele Wurme soll mein Leib erndhren,
Die reine flamme, die soll Verzehren,
Ich liebe slets die Warme und das light,
Denn verbrennt und begrabt mich night.

The translation is as follows:

Not one worm shall my life approach
the pure flame shall I make sure of
I love the state of the heat and light
Then don't burn and bury me.

Their own Viking death by the old Gods was even denied to them. The ghosts of battle became their own executioners. Triumph over the evil shells and the darkness was ours.

We looked towards the safety of the camp which looked a lot better and saved for us; hurrah for that!

The gates were opened for us in absolute silence like entering into another world of better things to come, raised above the land in its forward looking glory and victory for the downtrodden slave kind, a Calvary hill of crucified and Spartan perseverance against all oppression and the biggest odds history had ever known. The new Israel of all nations was born within the new man.
Two bombs had fallen one in front of the crematorium and one at the rear, but then again the symbol of our incarceration and inhumanity inflicted by man to man was still intact as an awful warning for everybody in defaulting over the coming of the Lord's promise to mankind, the coming of the savior, and don't do to others what you don't like done to yourself.

Keep the Commandments in your mind and soul for it to go well with you, rejoice. This is the covenant and vow to all God's people, old or new, Jew or Gentile, orthodox or free.

There is no preference, because they have all sinned, repented and been forgiven. We will have to reconcile and rebuild but our experience will have to help the stream of thoughts and influence the new man.

That is the aim of survival by the strong to the weak and to himself.

In the evening we would burn our dead and the flames from the ovens in Buchenwald for this once would go as high as those in Auschwitz but not to the glory of the murderous S.S. and Nazi hierarchy but to our salvation.

This would be our epitaph "To Each His Own" and we would stand on the appeal looking into the flames in memory of so many good and absent friends, some brethren, as in a last farewell to our misery in arms.

The tree of Goethe was blown over in the blast and laying on its side, prisoners cutting pieces of wood out of it for making souvenirs. Another prophecy and revelation had come to pass which was when the foliage starts to die the thousand year Reich was near to its downfall. When the tree would tumble over, close at hand, such was the strength of our faith. This had come to pass and was happening now. Above all human endeavors. God only helps those who help themselves. All

155

those sayings were going into action and fulfillment at the right moment.

The S.S. left us pretty much along for those three days of rest, we burned our dead and they tried to give the few of their important fallen figureheads a silent lugubrious ceremonial re-burial, a demoniac *Te Deum*, substandard with the weird funeral music that we could hear on the distant vibrations of the more purified air, quasi mystic more like black magic rites and very unpleasant to the ears. From their preoccupation with the occult they were burying their in- sanity, void of light understanding and pity.

We took advantage of this opportunity and managed to augment the supply of arms, hidden under the provision cart, coming in on the food run from Weimar passing along the ruins. This was helped by the total destruction and temporary setback on their iron oaths and crumbling discipline having received a lot of hard punches, right on in full face.

In Weimar we heard the people had heard the noise of the bombardment better than us and it gave them a prelude of what was in store for them.

After the third day the S.S. monster came back into its own but something was lost forever, they pulled themselves together again but it would never be the same, the stature and bearing was one, the creation of clay drying up and the reflection as well. Regarding the hiding of the arms, hardly anybody knew, not even myself. That was the sole responsibility of the elders of the camp as was the radio. Eight prisoners had given their life for that, taken at random after the raid, taken to Weimar for interrogation, tortured and vanished from the scene, without talking. We still had our secret as a last resort at the appropriate time, nobody was able to interfere with that, for himself or his buddies, this was for the whole camp and a divine rule.

Just like the landing or the final advance no selfishness or expediency would make the overture. So it was of no consequence that the dirty tongues were wagging afterwards, once and for all we can forget that, by the achievement of what followed and credit must be given, I hope, for it is a long time overdue on that subject.

The S.S. had a love affair with death and carried it on its wings. They knew, like Hitler, they were destined to be offered on the altar for their own iniquities and thus would take as many with themselves as they could to those killing fields before they also went. Hitler being the arch type of this like Nero.

They would still love to save their own skin if humanly possible, that went before everything and yet they were so close to corruption during their short existence on this earth. The knowledge of anything else would be a lot of speculation with such little evidence and a lot of guesswork to go on, much beside the point, creation is as it is much to our surprise. We are still practical creatures just the same and so it came to pass that the hiding place for everything was really under the chair, desk and floor of the S.S. doctor, a Bavarian in the "Ranken-Revier", the small row of first aid barracks stretched along near the fence on the left on entering the Camp.

All the time he had been playing a double role; from sending us on death transports to participating in single and multiple murders committed in the camp he was culpable as any other S.S. and at the same time tried to save his own skin. He had been taken in complete confidence by the camp elders, the all-German seniors. I don't know when exactly, it was before my entry anyway.

The radio must have been there too and honestly most of us didn't know, we couldn't even look the fellow straight in the eyes, it was best we didn't know him at all and vice-versa but what was certain quite a few were saved from the worst transports by his intervention.
After all these events we kept to our Commando's again as before, for a time we held our respective old places once in existence and collected screws and bolts to pile them in heaps, moved bricks back and forward, planks etc. and went to sit for a while on top of unexploded bombs to be left alone or have a tranquil rest.

Tom Mix was still doing his rounds with a whiplash now doing homage to his nick-name. One day a proud S.S. again, was walking past the shouldering covers of the Jewish shoes stacked up on the road when the damp heath, now revived by the breeze blowing reached an incendiary stick still hidden in it, and it went off suddenly and his pride went flat in the mud with his face in front of us all.

Aware of our presence, we just went deeper into the bomb pits, all he could was to try and gather himself together; we suddenly heard the gradual noise of shouting and the hollow sound of prisoners hammering on anything they saw to warn us of danger. It was Tom Mix, in all his glory, he had unexpectedly disappeared in front of us and fallen crosswise, stuck firmly wedged in an open crevasse not too far away from our position.

Nobody dared to go anywhere near him, he had managed to get his luger loose and screamed the more for it, announcing "Vervloechte Franszosen", all French for and us too, the row of bullets were for them and the last one for himself when it came to it.

Being drunk and afraid now that we would get him in his awkward position he kept us at bay. He eventually got out without help but in the evening he would be ready wielding his   whip   before the signal for stopping and entering the camp, after his   laughable debacle. Thus we got used to his capers after a while although he was still dangerous and still to be taken very seriously, better to be careful than sorry.

As winter approached we managed to gather enough planks from   the debris to make a fire, nobody stopped us anymore. I had the opportunity after a good warm up to explore further into the ruins and places never before seen so secret were heap they. I came upon a big heap emitting a lot of simmering heat and I had a good warm up with other prisoners from there about and looking around turning to all sides to get the best warmth all over my body. Suddenly my eyes noticed giant cylinders lying flat. I started to count them but the inmates from this department said simply that there were eight, obsolete and useless rockets without their spare parts to complete the assembly. Also the transportation was completely disrupted.

They would gradually be removed when repairs had been done, but for the moment definitively out of the war to destroy everything in their way coming down from the high altitude indicated. Those   were the latest secret weapons namely the V-2 in all their past glory now just scrap. One of the secrets that was held up until the full scale bombing took place with the impact and after our couriers had reached the Allied Headquarters via Switzerland. So that's what all the fuss was about.

The importance to be frank had never been so vital and in need of communication as this to succeed and we hardly had heard of it then as now. That was not all, the biggest of them all in line with the old Big Bertha fashion of 1914-1918 style, came to us and all, where a French pilot that I knew and with another group   from   my former transport arrived one day back most of them to die from tuberculosis or the miner's disease of silicosis or thysis, to my block, so we heard the whole story of the all famous D.O.R.A. "Deutshe Oberlander

Rochetten Aktiengesel-shate". (German Over-lander Rockets Company) It was of course a German ballistic missile enormous in size for a special long distance target, maybe London or New York, but wherever its destination would be, for a last big destruction and killing, so we had to stop it. That was our pigeon and so it was of the highest priority, and our efforts and secrets would be in service to this fulfillment: the destruction of this project. The Pilot told us how they had to work day and night in the most appalling conditions to fulfil this programmed tunneling in a primitive way, the machinery completely inadequate for nonstop work inside a long ridge, dying and dropping down like flies with it, beneath as well as above, walking miles to do their burrowing like the moles then from their camp.

A lot of experts were brought in once the silo was up and the gigantic rocket started to take shape like a big monster; can you imagine an atomic bomb in this nose cone or even enough explosives what a destruction that hellish contraption would have caused, maybe they couldn't exactly hit Times Square but they could hit New York from anywhere waiting for the moment they still had the capacity but not the time, it was running quickly out for them and the boycott and the messenger that had to go out for the project so that the Allies could annihilate it along with the V-2's.

A combine of individual acts was set in motion by a chain-reaction of diverse unplanned to planned operations which brought these results that would quicken the downfall of this evil genius or rather fool in his last efforts to burn Rome.

The information given by us was essential to start the process of intelligence concerning the V 2's, V-3's and military installations for jet planes down in the valley.

There were enough weapons there to have a ball with. "Peenemunde" was a baby by comparison. Nevertheless it was only *Peenemunde* that was ever mentioned out of it all.

Buchenwald is only known for its atrocities like any other camp, no recommendations for the action and deeds mentioned in this narration which were of the greatest importance to the cause.

The question of course why destroy a £50,000 epic when you could make the two combined without losing any credulity and please an intelligent audience with a masterpiece. If you have got to squash or destroy a good film after the war in the process of something that is

159

very wrong or else giving credit to any nation or nations or peoples, besides your own, is that it! One can do better than that. A further course of events would explain that, just like Buchenwald had a veil hanging over it.

My further explorations on the spot had me caught in one of the underground tunnels near the V-2's by meeting up with another S.S. this time a completely different experience!

Opposite to the other one and character as well than   the   one that beat me last time, the change was so great that I still wonder whether he was one of us or just monitoring the place after the bombing, disguised, whether they would have to hide their target once more.

As a matter of fact it looked as if he was hiding just as much as I was, disguised as an S. S. not looking for me. He was a gentleman, had class and was genuinely concerned about my welfare. He advised that it was better not to hide there and let me go unscathed, I never saw him again either.   The S.S.'s were operating inside now, taken from emigrant settlers from the U.S.A. with German origins.

Anyway no further communication were tried, this one was a purely coincidental nature. If he was an S.S. then things were really on the turn, but then again their blend was such that they could hardly change taken on their oaths and so called honors of the new knight's class, he didn't belong one bit to the lower echelons of brutal bullies we knew but was every inch an aristocrat in his bearing.
In the camp events were rapidly changing too. Criminals were completely eradicated from our ranks and the political taking over, to become Capos.

This was also the last time the gallows were being brought out for a public hanging as an example to us all in case we should think of trying to escape.

We had to watch for a couple of hours while the music played and the fellow, a Russian or Polish I think, was slowly hanged up and left to die, everybody was compelled to look upon it during that time. His executioner, a S.S. gave a speech about daring to escape and that was it. I always thought that there were two that I saw but from where I stood I had a rather awkward view and what with moving about, the helpers and the posts my view from the distance was somewhat impeded.

Winter went by in snow and freezing temperatures and I had the only woman's fur coat in the camp, it kept me decently warm, it was a bit thin and worn out but kept out the freezing wind very well, it also covered up my escape outfit, my hair was nearly normal now, no brush cut to spoil the effect.

The winter was made harder because of the long roll calls, we had to be counted and recounted until late into the night, they always found mistakes to be dealt with, unless the S.S. was a slow poke and we all came quickly to the conclusion it was really sour grapes because of the many setbacks they had now to face.

All their fronts were crumbling even the home front but even then they had to preserve their own institution as long as they could and we were the shield in front of them they could use and finish with them falling behind it, taking us with them. That was the intended finale; our sole hope was in this steam roller tactic to get and receive help from our Allies. Churchill had refused the arm drops we had asked for in return for the destruction of the secret arsenal. This would have given us the chance of an equalizer we had hoped for. It was not given because the answer was the reprisals on the other camps would have been terrible, he Churchill thought for the rest. That I leave to everybody and "To Each his Own" to digest.

Wing Commander Yeo Thomas had his reservations too, although he was saved by the camp resistance, very much like myself, for its uses so we have our reasons.

Because that is how he escaped death at the hands of the Gestapo and Nazis, not otherwise as the film suggested from the death transport. The camp saw to that and he could save no more of his buddies than we could save ours, when it came to the facts, or take the few weapons over with its Command on a flimsy superiority which no ordinary man possessed, as a matter of fact many of the inmates were more like cabbages than anything else and could also not get away from the death transports, if you didn't refuse near the end to leave the camp, all by yourself, this was challengeable and dependent on luck.

The Commandant by all kind of ruses over the loudspeaker tried to get as many out as he could to offset the pressure and shoot them down more easily later.

Weapons at that time would have meant massive suicide because the allies were still too far away and the Nazis to strong and therefore the suggestion of Yeo Thomas would have even made the general position worse. We cannot judge history on the statements of a few individuals, we were also still very much divided and it would have created an abominable state of armed suicide. This type of action was close at hand with the S. A. S. type we probably could have made a go of it with the weapons in our hands. I admire his courage above all, because that is the way I felt myself all the time and there was support amongst us but we hardly knew each other. The Underground was above it all and giving out the orders.

Churchill and the Allied Headquarters had made the right decision probably, but that is not how we felt at the time, I think we could have done better from our stand. Forgiving and accepting the facts is more useful than these silly accusations, jumping at each other's throats serves no purpose. I demand a new evaluation be made about this epic to put the events into their proper perspective in memory of this great sacrifice, it is Never too Late.

In-between those long roll calls on the Square and people starting to collapse around us I listened to some other groups present and one of them was a German Religious Sect of the latest Jehovah's Witnesses of whom I had heard very little.

Most of them seemed to be the offspring of the old Huttites from Sudetenland and Bohemia having lived in this kind of concept for a long time. Their faith and endurance was strong and persistent. They were stoic people and had suffered extreme cruelty from the beginning when the Nazis had meted out punishment to try to make them change their minds, their treatment was just as bad as ours and their numbers had been depleted enormously by it.

They were busy lecturing amongst themselves at the moment and the conclusion was that despotism was the result of the three organized evil forces ruling the earth, politics, religion and business; in other words absolute power, expedient hypocritism and unlimited greed. This was ruling the earth in their responsive personification of all evils, as the old devils or satanic forces. Therefore those forces would concentrate on opposing all that stood for good and enlightened behavior, and Vice Versa the good forces representing positiveness had but one duty to fight the negative ones.

They refused to fight against anything which was a complete controversial turnabout. The Lord or we had to do the fighting for them, the Creator of all and everything, very difficult to comprehend but their faith was constant with a core of mutual faith in study and belief and it was unique. I find those sects to be parasites but the study of the word does well. Everybody was doing the fighting for them.
If nothing is done about cleaning the total corruption and degeneration as in the balance of nature and sorting out the pollution of overproduction what or who does?

All that has to be done for progress and survival. Anyway their prophetic message was beware of the three forces set against you that they were talking about so widely. For any further enterprise this would always be a very strong influence and remain with my thinking, as it turned out more often than not until further enlightment. Nobody took them very seriously and it takes all kinds to make a world.

Snow and sleet was the pattern of the days and   nights and we were glad to get some sleep and rest when we returned from those long roll calls.

Janeck said he would find something better for me to do through his group organization and he did, so I got picked out for commando "Valkenhof", looking after the deer, boar and falcons in cages. This park was outside of   the fence and run by two German greens, or criminal youngsters of which I   didn't know anything at all, they were not Capos or anything but had this job for themselves alone. The animals were fed better than us and whatever was for them we had our fill as well, first on the side or at the end. This was rice custard in porridge from the elite S.S. The other was from all the S.S. kitchens and quite alright. The criminals were used to getting the extras and smuggled the stuff in for the Polish barracks where Janeck was.

One day as we got the barrels from behind the kitchen to load on to a small cart, which they let me pull alone, two S.S. passing by told them to give me a hand, looking at the different badges, and made sure that they did so. They didn't take to kindly to this; we arrived at the pen to feed the boars with it, and the scenery around was like a Wild West setting for taming wild horses with a beautiful view over the big open country, south, towards Erfurt. I was told to climb over the wooden fence to fill their troughs or feed boxes to the brim in between charges of those wild boars that seemed to enjoy the game, whilst the criminals passed the bucket from the barrel every time to me enjoying it too.

Those animals had very sharp horns protruding and took pleasure in running after each other, the entire circle just giving me a quick glance and a chance to jump over and back down the fence every time. Eventually I managed to get the damned box filled up to everybody's delight and by now I was panting for breath. After that we had lunch in a very nice cozy little log cabin, telling stories. Why didn't we escape from that corner? Easier said than done, the new young S.S. recruits were continuously training in those bushes and a bit further on, the watchtowers, that were in view kept a close eye on us.

One must not forget that those watchtowers were a bit like a fortress, on their own, manned by three S.S. constantly in three shifts, so we were being observed all the time. As previously pointed out there was also a training of guards and patrols with dogs going around the fence, our chances were slim.

In an emergency, the Tank Corps Panser Grenadiers below the hill near Weimar, could put a cordon around the base too and there were the farms with their Home Guards with dogs. The chances of any such attempt from here was just about one in a thousand so hardly worth the effort.

One day while I was still there as I was watching an S.S. column going down near the far corner of the fence, suddenly I saw a lonely Allied plane approaching as if from nowhere, probably looking for something worthwhile to hit. He must have come from the coast scanning along the wild parts and quickly dropped a couple of bombs and I think damaging the fence, no prisoner was ever in that corner anyway but the temptation would have been great for a quick breakaway. The S.S. were gone, I didn't see any of them anymore as if they had disappeared into thin air. The two criminals coming out of the block hut found me reappearing from one of the animal troughs a bit higher up and covered in fodder to their great amusement.

In the Camp, I found a couple of late arrivals caught in that bombing in the month of August both from the White Brigade, the Resistance in my home town of Ostend, old released soldiers, one was a well-known soccer player, goal keeper; the other his mate. The farmer's foot was wounded by shrapnel and the fellow had risked the run towards the S.S. barricade in the bushes and had been shot in the process. Similar to myself, the bullet had passed his hipbone, just a flesh wound and healed quickly as he was still a newcomer and better nourished.

The time of arrival here was a big thing in the survival rate. It was at this time that we laid our hands on special hostage letters or "*shultzhaffling*", issued only for them, mostly for the musicians, I should think, enabling me to send some news home and even asking for a few underclothes and a pair of leather shoes. Caniuz, a Belgian, part of our resistance group here organized it and translated in perfect German the written word. I think he owned a company of bookstores in Belgium. If in the letter we asked for too much it wouldn't pass the censor and certainly no food could be asked for.
The clothes could pass as they were for something called   gymastics, the shoes were a bonus all for the holiday camp.

I couldn't believe my eyes when I received them they were new I was still alive and had proof of where I was, that was the big bonus. For many of my fallen friends the parents wouldn't even know where they died and it would be an awful job to ask us how they spent their last moments.

Like the time when I was in a bad snappy mood from stress and quickly aging here. I answered so once on a Belgian's continuous question on my return in the evening from our commandos, asking how and what the news were, a common remark, and when the war would   be finished, and I responded back with a short angry "23rd of August" and he looked at me with such a pitiful and pleading   look, as if I shouldn't have said so. Such a damned glance it was with all the sorrows of the world embedded into it and I was now wondering on this. I kept to myself and was silent for a couple of minutes and afterwards said I was sorry. This was on the same day that he was killed in Steinbruck during the bombing; I had foreseen his end.

The S.S. building remained intact because the wave had fallen in front of it and the other wave past it, right in the quarries and made a real havoc, playing billiards with rocks and boulders, the effect was double of course and no chance of escape, Steinbruck was the grave of many prisoners and that was his destiny as well. He was a late arrival and still directed to hard labor in it, the place becoming his stone monument.

Al though we had succeeded in our aim to get Buchenwald bombed with the Allied help, my escape attempt was not over yet. The Resistance would still help me to get away as I was now ready so I got put into their commandoes and I lost track of "Valkenhof" soon after.

I managed to build my strength up a bit more that was the idea of the food.

The Resistance insisted on arms being dropped, as the armies where enclosing now and getting nearer to us. They didn't trust the intention of the S.S. regarding us when it came the crunch at the last moment. The extermination of us all was still on their priority list.

Our aim was to expand and to hang on as long as we could with the small amount of weapons we had, in the hope of holding out until the armies could rescue us.

Most of our former transports were sadly depleted to a ridiculous level, but the whole assembly of the late transports together amounted to a considerable number and would not be easy to handle: it would be a mammoth task to entice these people to revolt for us, as a matter of fact it could only be started by the resistance groups alone fully committing themselves openly. Only determined leadership was capable of such action if it had to occur.
Eventually the resistance had me transferred to Weimar police garage on transport to make a getaway.

I was given a briefing of how and what to do to save myself there, somebody would look after me there with my little bit of knowledge gained in Trade School for welding and mechanical aptitude, it would work out given a chance. If not I would be assisting around the shop somehow. I was convinced many of our leaders were also secretly Masons involved and after a while they had found it too risky, worried of being watched and given away in the shop. The German police officer in charge of the garage, a friendly man would try to get me into the "Veruretung Ban", the police headquarter used for wounded S.S. as a rehabilitation center.

Weimar was bombed regularly every night anyway. Every morning after we arrived under the watchful eyes of the security guards with their dogs, the town looked a little more different after a raid.

Parachuted mines had knocked whole rows of houses away causing devastation and demoralization.

The weather was becoming nippy at the time of our early commando. One morning a new jet fighter zoomed noisily over our heads, we thought it was something from another world, it was too cloudy to make anything of it but the noise and speed was speaking for itself. Just like Auschwitz we don't always have to see exactly to observe true happenings, it was there alright!!! I would say we barely had a glimpse. With all these changes and happenings the year was quickly coming to an end for all of us.

I helped with the cleaning of the classrooms, kitchen and store rooms, it was a police college used for S. S. invalids, with limbs missing and the handicapped people from the front who were studying new strategies on a blackboard visible to me.

One day I saw the VonRunstedt attack plan in chalk drawn on the blackboard mostly pertaining to the proposed campaign after a certain lecture. In the kitchen a very young Polish chap, friend of Janeck was in charge and the go-between: the Police, the Camp S.S. and the prisoners. There were also foreign workers, girls and woman doing the cooking all of them from the Eastern lands: Poland and Byelorussia mostly.

Our Polish connection and charge hand arranged everything from obtaining bread, potatoes and vegies.

On the bread-run, arriving for the store, he would have us in a chain-gang getting the single loaves passing them along from the cart outside, turning the stair and putting them on the shelves in the cellars below, quickly removing one from each shelf to replace the previous days one while the guard was still counting them; as long as he didn't go back to count the first lot, which he did once and got a funny answer as he burst out laughing. The two guards could never follow all of us at one and same time when it came to carrying the heavy baskets in. At the end he threw one or even two behind the door when we were lucky.

Everything was done so fast with him quickly passing the guards at lightning speed and us responding on a single command as he swished by.

We were never short of bread with him. Under our coats it went to take into the camp to share with our comrades in the block; first come first served. This helped the whole situation while I was working on my getaway. On the hill or rather curving ramp a bit further on was a slope running just above us where the trains, arriving or leaving from the other points westward would be slowing down enough to enable me to jump on it. I could make that at a good speed and pace being a fast runner, a bit off form and weaker but still good enough.

We were going out during the alarms here too. The Camp elders didn't have to encourage me much they knew that I would take it at the right time with a bit of calculation for the most opportune moment.

I got to know quite a few new arrivals in the camp especially in my block of which Antonio became an intimate friend of mine, he was Jewish, his father turned up a bit later, all former Spanish refugees from the civil war and now residing in Brussels in exile. Antonio had been involved in running the blockade over and back into Spain, with different businesses which he kept very silent about but which formed an integral part of our set-up in the war effort and the allied intelligence.

I believe him to being "Cato", code name for a Spanish operator from Catalonia, who had presented himself to the British Embassy in Madrid but first of all had been refused. His father was a Mayor of one of the suburbs in Barcelona. This Cato had offered his services then to all other intelligence organizations involved and then had gone back to the British giving false information to the Nazis.

Camuz was Russian intelligence and Wing Commander Yeo Thomas British Intelligence was given the code name "Nathan" in Buchenwald. A Belgian dentist, Mr. De Wever, "whigade" was from Antwerp and looked after me in my bloc especially as I was being framed by a German criminal stealthily filtered into the camp trying to accuse me of stealing bread from my fellow prisoners, after an unhappy incident I had with him about our place at the table and him threatening me, he was going to get me for this, in a moment of spiteful anger. It was in the nature of a very personal conflict becoming an enraged passion play, irritated who knows why by reaction to his provocation as he turned out to be a suspected ferret, as was found out later.

In his eagerness to frame me he placed my hat near the cupboard where the bread was missing with the inference of course that I was the culprit, it was too obvious to be true. Meanwhile the group proceeded to set a trap for him as for the rat that he was and it was much better done. I was still under stress, and the worry and trouble over this took over my plan of escaping and I caught a virus at the same time. I started feeling very sick with a high temperature. I had caught typhoid fever, having climbed over the dead and dying, the remnants of Auschwitz arriving from a last transport from there, quickly gathered due to the imminent and rapid Russian advance; "A forgone conclusion".

This poor residue of human survivors just came and expired in Buchenwald, their conditions being appalling, dying and lying in their own excrement in specially fenced off areas, the Germans were afraid to catch the diseases too, typhus, dysentery and diarrhea.

Well, I had caught the lot I guess, what a moment, they all thought I was a goner; I was delirious. Spiritually I was far away from worldly surroundings, light came in though by my over sensitiveness of presences which I had not contemplated before, clearly visible and heard by me in a state of trance I would say; one of course thinks straight away at hallucinations caused by my sickness, it probably helped to make me comatose, yes, but not a coma or without cause, what they call the twilight zone, the ethereal, not quite the astral, when one leaves his body, but maybe just before and being fully conscious, not during any sleep either !

It was late in the evening when I got up from my bunk more by force. We had a night guard on duty amongst us, who was out of the dormitory. I saw the door opening from his side and a person entered and put something in the bin, I saw it clearly from the inside and in between the artificial light zone, a person which I recognized as having been killed the previous day by the Yugoslavs, a traitor for Michaelovitz, Tito's partisans they were !

None of us interfered in the affairs of others that was theirs alone. The unhappy spirit that he was came back clearly as if he was there in reality and obviously was bothered about something that he had left undone, maybe to help me in my troubles, who knows, possibly he was innocent of the crime. I went to the Guard in the anteroom which was our communal dinin hall, and he said he had seen nothing, and anybody entering there whatsoever had to pass him.
Still very much under the influence of this strange phenomena we began a conversation on a wide variety of subjects of which I was quite knowledgeable and very accurate in an answer to his question as to when the war would finish: Pressure was rising around me to a high

level and I could hear rattling and hissing noises making an awful din behind the door of the dormitory; I threw the door open to quell them and some of the elders came out and tried to subdue me instead even to the extent of one of them stabbing me with a sharp object in the neck!

They couldn't hold me at all. I had to much superior strength than them combined, again, nothing could hurt me. I mentioned the noises now which they   didn't hear and   couldn't understand. To me they were personalities and beings and I had to follow them more as of a certain substance than the ones I left behind in this life shaking   their head now. The noise let me straight to the bunk of Jose DeWever the Belgian Dentist who was fast asleep on the top of the three rows in his bunk.

I climbed that and nobody was following me, probably wagging their head still in utter disbelief and thinking it was my fever making me crazy, that was only the contributory factor, I had to do so to relieve whatever had set me to this.

I knew we had to have help beyond the normal to get this problem solved, this ferret criminal was a grave danger to us all. He would have given the lot away.

He knew too much about all of us, that's for sure, this was a climax being played out. Anyway as I reached the top I touched   DeWever and as soon as I did that, the whole effect left me and I relaxed, it was done, my peace of mind returned. The following   morning they caught the culprit and I never saw him again!

The fever had left me although I was still a bit wobbly. Somebody told how he had changed his triangle and infiltrated into our section but Jose DeWever had done all the investigation. Soon after this incident I returned to the center in Weimar but the impetus of my escape was somehow taken away from it all and I remained, maybe for the better.

Janeck's friend started a love affair with a German girl which was very well known to all of us and successful also, the Germans close by us liked it. We all seemed to idealize and support the secret romance and protected the smooth running of it.   Sometimes they had long moments by themselves during the alarms that came more frequently than at any other time.

One day we passed along a river with a big ridge rising just behind us. We had stayed out much longer than the usual time and I also noticed two very fit German S.S. with an amphibious "Volkswagen", a short distance away from me, they seemed to be   putting something down near the fence very laboriously with great concentration and then they drove quickly away, in an awful hurry   they were.

The next day the same long alarm occurred again and lingered on too. This was the 9th of February 1945 on a clear and beautiful sunny day, a bit chilly that was all, but very dry and we were enjoying our outings: All of us standing in a group talking together when all of a sudden from behind the ridge, on an average attacking altitude, the super fortresses appeared in full formation for the now usual occurring   frontal assault throwing their smoke tracers, at a steep angle, down, in various colors to see better. The big prelude had started, we just saw the released bombs beginning to drop awkwardly out of the opened bays after this a draught and hearing a horrible noise we realized that they were coming straight towards us, the sound waves being dissipated above our heads. Holy mackerel, we had just about time left to run and jump quickly behind the parapet bordering the river when the impact hit the ground where we had just been standing, the mud and stones falling all around us and into the river, one very sharp stone piercing the front of my cranium, with blood spurting out and down my face, it was a small sharp deep cut as if by an arrow head.

Around the edge of the nearest enormous crater was one of my mates laying without any movement just behind the turned over edge of it. We felt for sure that he was dead, when suddenly he woke up and rose as if from the grave and joined us, smiling, if ever I saw a Zombi like creature that was him, maybe everything just passed over him. He was one of the surviving carpenters and builders left behind in Buchenwald. The Angel of protection or the crossing of the Red Sea in small doses was happening to quite a few of us or we liked at least to think so for our own sake. Otherwise the dividing line was very thinly strung. When would all of this stop, we had all had about enough by now.

The landscape was changed into a real mess, the earth overturned and poles and ruins left behind with all kind of debris being strewn about, mixed up, making it look like a tornado had struck, earthquake and battle, everything having raged in one hell of a havoc a complete chaos.

We had no intention of returning to the center as the as the sound of heavy planes kept on, and on turning around and returning to look again to see if there was anything worthwhile left. Our guards had had enough of it as well. Everybody just walked away, what a pity there were no trains available at such a moment. They were either out of service, hiding or destroyed. The only thing that we could do was look around and we saw an outstretched S.S. killed by a huge concrete slab jettisoned right on his chest. He couldn't have been deader, we put him carefully on to a stretcher with changing the pole bearers alternately and followed the cartage out, that was our safeguard against any further complications. We caught up with our guards further along near a village and a ravine and they asked us what is that that you are carrying there, and when we told them, they said, throw him into the valley and good riddance.

From this ravine civilians started appearing in bunches now as the planes had finally gone and looking at us and office, for a minute, they got a bit worried and then in confidence they told us, you do not look like terrorist at all, the Nazis made us believe all that crap.

We helped them to get over the last steep edge with giving them a hand to pull themselves up and out and we were taken back in trucks provided for us, all the way back to the camp. I do not know why, maybe from now on we were safer in the camp against mob violence and attacks or meeting up soon with retreating troops and S.S. squadrons on revenge raids. This is why the planes concentrated on this place, Weimar became the cross roads of the German retreat now.

I also think that the two S.S. men that I had noticed the previous day, before the bombing, with their Volkswagen had planted something there near to the fence to attract attention. I do not what, but something that helped to guide the planes, again they were not S.S., most likely S.O.S. surely they were infiltrators. I was so convinced of it that it made more confident that the camp would be saved as well and I was thinking lesser now than before of escaping, that wouldn't had been very wise, all things considered. On the other hand never under estimate the strength of the S.S. or their capabilities. On the night of the twentieth to the twenty first I felt very disturbed again, I knew that something horrible was going on, my senses were acute all the time, I was sitting up again in the dining hall talking to the night watchman we kept inside, when an old S.S. crept in, known as the hangman from his patrols among the barracks.

He warned us not to risk ourselves by going outside for any reason at all. It was the night of horrible executions in the cellar of the crematorium on all the families of the plotters. Wholesome German families were actually being murdered there by the S.S. as accomplices and for treason against Hitler. This proved that the little mad corporal and his blind followers had still enough power to do what they liked and mete their vile retribution out accordingly in blood curdling tortures. So much the more reason for us to beware and to be ready at all times. Wing Commander Yeo Thomas and a contingent of a dozen British with twenty three or more French and Belgians, all S.A.S. Special Air Service, had come in too then, most were from the Channel Islands, fully bilingual and all considered as terrorists and agents on Hitlers specific orders and radio broadcasts which he had recently made. I remember it was near the end of August 1944, after the bombing of Guzloff exactly that they appeared, brought in quickly on the advance after the landings, and also when Antonio came on the scene.

The film made in his honor "Sentenced to Die", from the same book of the "White Rabbit" was shown only once for a selected audience and then destroyed, a £50,000 epic acted by Kenneth More as Wing Commander Yeo Thomas; Why? It was going to be shown around the Commonwealth then.

14- Last Days of Buchenwald:

During the last days of Buchenwald, similar to Pompei, things just followed each rapidly in quick succession from the shooting of those S.A.S. inmates to the murdering of the rebellious few plotters and their families.

The big hulk of the hangman was always very near, on the occasions when something like that was going to happen, like an evil sighting of a banshee. I was not too far away from the shooting and executions, I was at that time, in the presence of a small German criminal notary, near some trees growing the much looked for triangle nuts we were nibbling on.

The butcher hangman told us to keep quiet, before we heard the shots, stroking his black moustache in consternation and deep concentration, to him it was a matter of a most serene ritual. Who was he after all? It was a bit more than just a job for this man. Why was he always appearing from nowhere on those moments? Before that I had never seen him anywhere. Was he like a counterpart of a fiddler on the Roof, softening the impact of tragedy? I was sorry for the fellow when I heard the rattling short bursts in quick succession, all was over them at the moment, the bravest.

I hoped somehow that my nearness would be of some help to them in their last moments as there was no priest amongst us!!!

Present with me also were two very frightened people from a little place in Belgium, a town Mayor and his helper, batsman I should say, as he was always with him trying to do things for him instead of looking after himself. The Mayor was old and starving after an opulent beginning and failed to survive the coming end of the war, the servant died in Belgium shortly afterwards broken hearted and dispirited. Those two were an inseparable pair and worked incessantly not daring to look up for one minute. I have seen twins die like this from our adjoining transports when in quarantine.

Before we were finally kept in the camp and all commandos stopped now I had a last outing to Weimar and found myself a bit further away than usual on a bombed out police station with adjoining stores to clear.

The damage had really shaken the old house to pieces, it was full of Masonic regalia and trinkets. It was a secret Mansion type of house till the end, that explains a lot, I could have hidden there somehow too, so a lot of our German inmates turned out to be ancient members from their outside connections, mostly in the police, so were the Belgians that had helped me and not all communists as some people would have liked to have made out. My own inclinations very much the same after war.

Across from this was the gymnasium or High School as they call it, we cleared and cleared that as well, it was full of 18th and 19th century dress uniforms. One day during an air raid warning we went far, over towards a local cemetery and the crematorium on a slope and saw the surrounding countryside, tombs were coming down near to us and a lone plane was busy strafing thing a bit further away, the total collapse seemed imminent by the state of things.

I found it more prudent to stay in the camp by now. I found a cigarette packet, probably old Turkish, with the 'Do Nife' written on it, which reminded me of my aborted mission. Reminiscence of (unclear word) where it had all begun, I was convinced that I would see her soon again and that she was safe and never been caught or given away.

The date was now the seventeen of March and the bombing of Dresden had started: super fortresses were flying nonstop over Buchenwald as if for orientation dropping their loads over the doomed city, landing in Russia and doing the same thing on their way back to the Island setting like an aircraft carrier. Day and night until the porcelain city was no more. We heard the distant rumblings and Coventry was avenged. A fire must have completed the rest similar to Hamburg's multiple bombing raids.

The camp was overflowing from the all over retreat: quick commands from the tower for faster executions was the routine of the day now and we were still waiting.

Many of the Germans went into hiding by mixing in with us and trying to prepare a place of refuge for themselves. Richard Thalman, they were after him soon enough and got him near the end just the same.

When transports were assembled the personal roll calls ceased, no more time for that, that is what we had waited for, our time was coming.

The Russian section went first, voluntarily, with the idea to jump their guard in unison on one signal, they did just that successfully and got away with it. There was no way that the guards at such a close range could take evasive action and shoot all of us, all the time I had known that but you must have the people to do it with. They offset some death transports which received the worst of it; instead of seeing it out with us Wing Commander Yeo Thomas rushed ahead which nearly cost him his life and he was later on picked up by an American advanced column from the many dead and dying.

The camp Commandant was even begging and lying to get us out, promising nice carriages, food etc. Now we could smile at last, we knew we had to refuse and stand up but not before they tried to make a last attempt to get us out with what force they had left. We heard on the loud speakers a croaking voice speaking quickly and saying: "*Schnell, Schnell!*" All to the assembly place, all blocks out! This was seven days before the eleventh of April, 1945.

No more food had come and we knew that the Americans were not too far off, the 8th Army, but not near enough yet. One old S.S. came storming down from the tower their pistols in hand shooting wildly around them. Screaming Jews first and anybody too slow or running back down to hide was shot at, so we had to walk very slowly up to the hated square. Their forces were very much diminished and that was their last show which was spread out to the most dangerous proportions.

Together with Antonio I carried his dad and between us we trailed a bit to long for our own good with the old man, he told us to let him go but we insisted while the shooting went on left and right of us regardless of our own safety. Now and then I glanced at the murdering going on. Eventually we joined the ranks to be counted for the last time now!!!

As an S.S. looked straight down the ranks to align us up, a Jewish prisoner moved along and put himself between us, Antonio and I, he was pushed by the others and would have fallen out at the end and been shot by the S.S. was it not for us covering him. Pleading he looked at Antonio and I, I'll never forget all this. Antonio was Jewish too but that was not known, but we would have been shot had they found him in between us. Not a word was said and the danger passed missing a potential victim, the retrieved man just looked at us and stayed with us for a while to disappear later.

176

Afterwards when they had their amount right they went out and we had another reprieve: we then descended to our blocks   determined not to get up   anymore, that was it, whatever was to come, and this was the finale, them or us.

Those were the survivors and fighters left amongst us, the weak ones and unfortunate had been sorted out but we were among a big pack of skeletons, an army of the walking dead. In the evening we stood watching the fighting going on and developing in the valley, what a spectacle that was, guns blazing spitting fire and brimstone, it was like a land and sea battle combined. People were still dying around us, en masse, I just had about eaten up all the little tit-bits I had saved for such an emergency.

The Danish police, remnants of a small rebellion started in Copenhagen, were dying like flies unused to the severe hardships of the extreme conditions that we had gradually adapted to. Red Cross packets for them had been divided and distributed to everybody at the last minute so the chances for all turned out to be more or less equal, as much as was possible, the donations were internationally divided.

I had the advantage of the former commando, the animal food from the pig trough that was a help plus those meagre supplies. All that we could do now was to sit and wait for the last orders, we were ready for action. The tension was growing and at last on the 11th of April we heard the tanks crawling up the hill, spotted planes flying over, those were ours anyway, clearly visible in the morning. The U.S.A.'s Eighth Army was on its way.

The watchtowers gradually turned their machineguns on the advancing army and assault troops coming steadily and stealthily up with the tanks.

That was the moment we all had waited for, when they were not enough and the sporadic firing started. Every block stormed out on a signal and was organized at a quick tempo by their already prepared commanders. I had Jemy Blum from Brussels as my leader; "You and you, there you go" no daubt or shaking of heads was tolerated, or stay behind he told the slackers, in this case speaking to a lawyer. It was four o'clock in the afternoon. The ones that didn't go for the fighting had to brake the chairs, stools and to pass the arms to us. White flags were put up in the blocks to avoid confusion and mistakes by the fighting forces. I was given two German stick grenades and told how to use them, putting them in my belt. Knives, pistols and a few rifles that was all we had.

Now everybody can observe why we couldn't have broken out before, it was negligible. We charged like mad bulls at the fence while the guards were battling with the Americans in front.

It only took a few grenades to get a gap in the fence and cut the electricity flow, throwing the rest in the watchtower from our positions and make for the S.S. arsenal in a hurry, that's where the weapons were; in no time we were armed from head to toe, a formidable determined small little army to account to. The diehard S.S. were killed where we actually found them, no chances were taken, in their fox-holes.

In all we took two hundred prisoners by ourselves, which was not a bad show, and we were able to hand them over to the Americans almost intact. Here and there, an individual bit the dust of course, that was understood. I found my mentor from beating fame, dead already in a fox-hole, fighting until the end.

He had chosen his way out and not otherwise. During the past day President Roosevelt had died and we made a last farewell ceremony in arms as a solemn tribute to him and what it all stood for, the final victory.

When I looked at our squadrons and their weapons it was an impressive crowd and a Farewell to Arms. Luckily most of the battle was over now, except for a few skirmishes, because as we later found out those big grenades on their sticky ends you might say, thrown by a strong spring when released, were much untried in the enormous rush and exploded more often than not. The operator was supposed to sit in a fox hole and then pop up and manage the thing. Anyway the spirit was there above everything else. A forerunner of the bazookas.

Some of our Germans went straight to their old homes, weapons and all were taken. Nothing was heard, everything was under control and orderly. Big sprees of revenge and retribution didn't occur beyond what one would normally expect in such circumstances. Talks with the townspeople took place on a grand scale. The only news of any importance was discovered by the Americans, at the last minute, an S.S. platoon was on its way to burn us out with flame throwers and was intercepted in a scissors grip, just in time.

Their intention was to trap us inside and then put fire to every block with their hellish flame throwers. Luckily we had our weapons because a real battle would have started, which we actually would have welcomed tremendously, after all, we had waited long enough for that fight with our cruel captors. Instead we were told food would come and first aid also and it was better to wait until all received relief and we would also be looked after for proper repatriation with identity papers after scrutiny.

15- Liberation:

Delegations, representatives of the Red Cross and others arrived and the Camp was laid open for general public inspection. Nobody could understand the evidence bared to their eyes. It was beyond normal reasoning and moral decency. The skeletons of dying people were still moving around for everybody to see, the mass graves opened and those people still piled up in the yard of the crematorium was incomprehensible to most.

Of course the pressure had been high near the end, nobody would deny that, but it was also only equal and parallel to former times when they were victorious and combined more killings in between times for longer periods than now, near the end.

There is no doubt about that the reasonable people, the mathematical figures speak for themselves, no matter how you got them. By your own account or with those little computers fed by so called intelligent people just as long as you know what you are doing.

I don't know what happen to the French president Leon Blum and his wife in their villa retreat or the numerous Rumanian aristocrats they just went back like us I supposed. Antonio and I had been once assigned in commando work over there and environs and we had seen some of these people.

We looked in amazement at the oven with the charred remnants that were left, especially when showing an American sergeant around in charge of the control commission on all camps as they open, like ours hi name was Elmer Luchterhand and he became a friend. Sgt. H.Q.Co., Inf, E.T.C., U.S.A. Army.

We also saw the lampshades made of human skin, the horrible little hobby of Ilse Koch, the wife of the commandant and also the shrunken heads, diver's masks, representing the different races of partially shrunken heads staring at you from the wall. One in particular took my attention and I recognized it, it was of a tall Cameroonian I had seen in Fort du-Ha or Caserne Boude. Different human parts were preserved in jars for multiple experiments, it was all there for the believers and unbelievers to gaze at. It still should be but I heard lately evidence is gradually disappearing. Madame Tussard had nothing on this, it was the real thing and a mind boggling experience for us all.

180

The hooks in the crematoriums were all covered up, about fifty of them freshly cemented in, all the evidence destroyed on the surface.

Another crematorium between this and the kitchen, with bigger foundations was under construction. They had, indeed great plans for the thousand year Reich, ambitious, continuous and of a lasting kind. There was a perfectly manufactured lift or elevator in good condition and working well, carrying the executed ones to the ovens, three powerful furnaces. Everything worked so smoothly all the time without many interruptions. The skull smashing mallet was laying nearby where they dropped it, some evidence for the victims, contrary that were still partly alive after the prolonged slow suffocation, or the strapping clamps or hooks, a last order if there were kicking stupors.

There was the whipping block, the ashes and partly burned bones and bodies everywhere. Unearthing a mass grave near the Bismark Tower was enough evidence as to what had happened to the transports that never got off and were cut out of hearing. All those places were opened and even Germans made to take a good look and do the digging back in or carrying the corpses.

I never saw Janek and many others again, only Antonio, his dad and Jose Dewever and a few others. I figure that 1200 to 1600 of my transport vanished as only two hundred survived.

You can think that was about the same for the other transports. The health of those few afterwards left much to be desired, a good deal of them died shortly afterwards, others handicapped and invalided. We weren't given too much food when we first arrived, weaned like babies I should say that was another hazard for our dilapidated bodies. Some people were worse than others of course.

Elmer Luchterhand, Antonio, myself and another prisoner had our photo taken at the gate for the watchtower with 'Jedem das Seine' by photographer Walter Poller. We stood just like the two bookends with Antonio and Elmer hiding behind the two in front. This was taken by Walter Poller first back there just after the liberation, a former German inmate. For his book 'Medical Block Buchenwald', after all this and when Elmer had told us to keep near to him and to the available for his report, he would take us away with him, in the meantime we had a through walk around the camp and scrutinized it carefully. Firstly we came across to funny fellows throwing combat knifes into a board inside at the bottom of a watch tower where I had once stood when they shut the S.A.S. men and eaten the beech nuts. As we were unarmed, ours have been surrendered to the new camp commandant of the U.S.A., the best thing was a hasty retreat we thought and I said to Antonio that they were S.S. disguised and not Americans at all, they hardly spoke to us.

Later under British army found the S.S. Koch, Commandant of Buchenwald in a prisoner of war camp disguised and Ilse much later received amnesty and was found to be pregnant, by who knows. So much for that, they were living it up, of course, the leniency of our judicial system and courts has also become our downfall and maybe what I don't know yet. All the people on the wrong side of the fence think that it is plain weakness anyway, so what are the odds and experience if we cannot change thinking; if certainly is not a course or is progress our upside-down psychology, no matter how many books are written. There is definitely not the slightest proof or truth in any of their philosophy but it gives it new science a favorite position to do a lot of writing, until we can replace by surgery or other methods or can remove this thing of our primitive mind in the construction of our makeup or brains I cannot see how they can do anything about it at all. That is my theory of the subject of what I have seen and concluded and is the only thing that seems to have any reality in it, the rest is humbug.

Having insatiable curiosity and enquiring mind we pursued our explorative walk much further afield after having worn some Americans of our intention and the two fellows we had seen.

The world was well satisfied that justice had been done at the Nuremberg trials and that topped the lot, has been a closed verdict on it all.

They would need some of them for their next competition and this would overshadow our respect for the rest of our lives I am   afraid in all kind of dark shapes, so would the other side pursue   the   same program. The moneys acquired from their more affluent victims would bring financial benefit and secret personal files made up would undergo the same cover up treatment for posterity. All that I can say is that I have been in Buchenwald.

In Bonn, Brussels and the Pentagon my files are, who knows where else, Whitehall and Moscow, maybe, but the most possible place is nowhere.

We just kept on walking like the wandering Jews did in some of our reincarnations I suppose, we must all have one or not, every religion believes so but at the same time I cannot make head or tail of all that even lesser than before. It is all very much like being left in limbo as some priest once said.

We were now descending into the forest now at the other side from the old quarry towards the open plain.

At the bottom of the hill near the farms we came across a funny haystack, sticking out like a thorn in the side in the middle field, and on the wind we smelt petrol fumes and human flesh. The S.S. had been around at work, no doubt, who else. I looked at the haystack again and said to Antonio "It seems too much of a set-up, probably an ambush, let's get out of here quickly before we get fried".

It was too early in the year to be there in the first place and the flat facade of the front was facing the road towards us and besides that I could feel the staring and being watched. Once behind the walls of the building we made our safe getaway, they wouldn't give themselves away either unless they had to, not wishing to attract attention to themselves, or by the time we could send help they would have gone anyway. On this little incident who wants to get shot at the last minute of hostilities or even after. Following our return from the vicinity of Weimar. Elmer came to see us announcing that he had a mission arranged and that everything was in order with his Commandant, he would take us and start a report. Antonio was a good hand at typing and I had all the information on Auschwitz and the extras.

Eisleben was from where Martin Luther was born, and that is where he took us. Sporadic fighting was still going on around us, pockets of them were holding out and we could hear the distant thuds, Elmer said so too and he kept running back and forth from those places. He had found an old farm house on the outskirts of the town, a typical old Saxon place with an old Aunt in it, having her relations and daughter there whose husband was a Nazi official she told us in confidence. This lady was very stuck up with the Nazi culture or niche as she, the Aunt, put it and had a lot of excuses to justify it.

Antonio and I told the lady where to get off. We didn't waste any time on her and got on with the job now as Elmer had brought a typewriter in. We lived on the same U.S.A. rations as him but the Aunt talked sometimes to us confidentially and gave some of her supplies whilst we were busy.

It was a very historical house and I wouldn't be surprised if Marin Luther hadn't visited it at least once as I said everything indicated a past era. The atmosphere was perfect for it, old musty furniture, chandeliers and Dresden china all over the place.
Antonio got himself typing away until very late in the night and we dropped off to sleep with sheer fatigue. I woke up very early in the morning, around four o'clock, wide awake with a strange overwhelming feeling of a strong super natural presence filling the room, the nearest to a light with Antonio still fast asleep. I was unable to reach him from my chaise longue I was resting on, the force held me back,I was in a state of rigid suspension and practically weightless at the same time: I had to concentrate now and stare at the center of the room looking up at the chandelier on the ceiling. I never had experienced anything like this not even during my fever, when a strong vibrating manly voice emanated from somewhere between the ceiling and chandelier filling the room. Antonio was helpless unaware and asleep at the time. Nothing seemed to exist around me anymore time and the visible world had stopped it was worthless.

The voice real very powerful was talking clearly to me in German, which I understood like my own language that was no barrier at all. A lot of the serious talk was the same warning and words I had heard from the students of German Bible a long time ago, when we were on the parade ground but much stronger and with a greater importance, saying "you will go around the world saying the things I want you to, for my sake, and three powers will always be against you in your endeavors, anybody shaking your hand first is not really your friend, watch out".

After that I went and relaxed, all my feelings returned and I was convinced about the reality of this power. It had been as if I was partially uplifted. I talked to Antonio afterwards about it and he said his Grandmother had experiences like that too.

From all the studies undertaken later there is only one conclusion of this interpretation: Some people are used at certain points in time for particular revelations. Their presence and thinking is vice versa, influential to the events. Having considered hallucinary influences from the abominable situations we found ourselves in and had to cope with

this was a different experience, the starvation, the stress and the sudden contrasts encountered make those
actions of the mind maybe more sensitive but is not necessarily the main factor. I think we all had a role to play with being there. At the same time I had my fever and recuperation after a smuggled in magnesium tablet of English origin came into my hands well before the collapse at the end. It told me of things to come in the stories that interested me most regarding us and the fall of despots in general throughout historical times.

From Constantine seeing the flaming cross in the sky to the fall of Byzantium with a copy of a most impressive painting I have never been able to find and and to crown I found indication that it was supposed to be in the national gallery in London, as untrue, unless it is the Tate gallery by now, I will have to enquire about this.

It pictured at turmoil very dark and stormy sky, Wagnerian in looks, whiling clouds passing by, chased by a roaring wind, lighting visible in the distance and depth, or rather abysmal, background in the somber valleys and seeing gorgeous of the far off foothills reminding me of my own in-depth look from Auscwithz to the Carpathians.

From this appears as silent terrible crowd of all kinds of sinister looking forces with wild eyes, war horses before the carnage of the battlegrounds starring hysterically with their pompous riders drawn from all the known faces in history sitting firmly in the saddle, just trotting with standards flapping away.

They were dignitaries, generals, popes, bishops, Caesars and conquerors of the most despotic nature known, you name it: Ramses, Nabuchadneza, Yerxas, Huniti, Attila, Napoleon and onwards to our little corporal Hitler, it was there. All walking and trampling over the mutilated and broken bodies of mankind.

The little children in Auschwitz, Treblinka, Rava Rutchka, Buchenwald and so many others, all crying 'look what they have done to us, tell the world please" so please it is not much to ask, hurry! On this revelation and true epitaph. Elmer gave us an authorization to return to Buchenwald with it, which he very well knew he will not do from now on. So all roads lead to Rome, ours was home to Belgium. From a convenient viewpoint he most have watched and observe us going the other way instead of Buchenwald, that was the last of it for us and what we saw of him.

He went straight for Eisenach instead of lower Franconia, using the oldest transport we could lay our hands on, from empty tank carriers which shook us inside and out, especially when traversing fields trying to avoid bomb craters pocketing the roads, to any left we could get.

In the process we eventually we picked up two British prisoners of war armed with a pistol for travelling with us then later on a sharp thin fellow who seemed to be disguised, a Nazi official I thought, dressed in an outfit which one assumed it to be Belgian wearing a beret like one sees in some British films, out of context, usually we do not wear berets like that, the Belgian colors were sown on it; with the first cross questioning he fell into the bag, completely, and he confessed to me that he couldn't deceive me, furthermore he was too perfectly supplied with a small carefully prepared rat pack which we gladly shared amongst us until we passed him over to an American Commandant camped along the road.

Soon enough he talked himself out of that one and the last we saw of him he was talking stealthily away across the fields with his sentimental photo of his wife and children, he could probably have been a Nazi like Eichman.

On a cross road all wagons and vehicles were collected and made to park in a field, the quantity getting bigger by the moment, traffic directed by a big Texas Ranger with a big cigar gesticulating wildly and showing them the way.

The oddest thing we had travelled on was a fire-engine! That took quite a lot of us. Here the great cross-road was for Frankfurt, heavily bombed enveloped in ruins, just walls and chimneys left standing upright, the inhabitants probably asking themselves whether it had all been worthwhile, yes it had, once it was started it had to be completed.

Soon we reached the old River Rhine which we crossed over on a pontoon bridge quickly built and from there we had already waiting a train to take us to the province of Luxembourg which placed us right in Belgium, near Arlon on our way to Brussels.

For the road we had plenty of good food, fish fruit and vegetables, drinks were provided. The German children were now the very willing receivers, no "Sour Grapes" here, a new generation of innocent and

"Ohne Michs!" Growing up instead. This was not repeated, "Only a dead Indian is a good Indian".

At Arlon we were also cleared by Security because everybody was with us as is the case with all refugees and the inherent problems. A tall woman was airing her patriotic feelings by declaring what we should do to the Boche. In the first place I do not like this name, calling all people alike after this infamous mass murderer is wrong in the second place, and for third place we will not go very far with such an attitude as proof we haven't learned anything at all from this.

A lot of people were waiting there in hope and more often in vain for their loved ones to come back.

Revenge wouldn't bring them back either, but hope may do it in a firm belief of a better world. Some fanatics would even arrive back in S.S. uniforms which hurt to hear of such a thing, their little souls had been so badly indoctrinated that they couldn't change. The maddened crowd would either lynch, drown them or chop their heads off before the law could stop them.

 It has to be understood how much more extreme aggravation could they take even by putting it down to simple mindlessness. Our arrival in Brussels went by unnoticed by all, nobody had expected us back like this. A reception party has to be prepared to be successful. I suppose we were quite happy to be back, in the first place that was more important. Within our ranks came an unknown factor who turned out to be an architect with the name of Francesco. All three of us found temporary shelter with my aunt Helen such was her genuine hospitality, until they found their own way about.

Francesco was soon involved in his traditional habitual impulsive plotting I should say, which we were not entrusted in at all. To this day I do not know who he was, an infiltrator? Antonio didn't like it either and soon Francesco disappeared out of circulation altogether working with the Italian Embassy officials. They both went their own way and were able at their own discretion to for fight for their existence, like myself.

Over their own experiences they liked to put a self-imposed state of amnesia as a cover, mostly I think because nobody could understand their plight and the inner conflict was too difficult to overcome. My opinion is, even if it has to take a lifetime to accomplish such against the continuously changing world values one has to have the strength to overcome and persevere, as in our case.

Now I understand more and everything fits at last in each other, like a puzzle. People like my sponsors formed an integral part of the last Empire to keep it together by their loyal and patriotic actions and positions attained, whether that was secret and official or completely on a voluntary basis makes no difference. It was just as effective and contributed to the whole. The same kind of mainstream and background would attract us to each other and we would be looking out for similar beings. In the camp the same secret combination would happen between the equal elements created that way and would therefore use each other as the only worthwhile strength, considering above that stood the divine works, in which we were merely the visible mediums and stern carriers as long as we lasted, but there would be unavoidable preferences in person.

So it was thus, we were all used, because we had something to give and the strength faith and stability to fulfill things and as such we were kept in abeyance for this purpose. "To Each His Own".

A tribute in revelation to the vindication of all survivors and an honorable memory to all absent brethren alike, who haven't departed in vain, I hope.

16- Repatriation to Belgium:

After a while we all returned, myself first, then soldier Barbaix and eventually Daniel from the East run away or rather escaped. The only thing we could think about was enjoying ourselves first of all but where was the money coming from that was the question.

I had just about passed our Control Commission, which decided who was a Political Prisoner and who was most certainly not, besides this, of the ten thousand genuine survivors there were ninety thousand impostors too greedy after the benefits we were going to get: all this prolonged our agony with endless waiting. The whole process was embedded in red tape and a noticeable opposition of reactionary forces from within.

Then there was the battle of the Government we had during the occupation and the one in exile. All this had to be sorted out by the competing factions or compromised eventually.

With the Kings question they made short measurement. Everybody agreed to it, that he should abdicate until his son was ready for the throne. In the meantime Prince Albert was his "Voogd". It was a moral and symbolic decapitation in fact for the King himself.

There were a few Political Prisoners that had seats in the Senate for the Government and also controlled some newspapers like Blum for the people. The rest was firmly united and organized in the Association for Political Prisoners. I remember demonstrations in the capital where we went, to hurry our cases up so that we could start with our civil normal lives again.

All this was gradually achieved mostly after two years with filling bags of papers up and being considered as demobilized soldiers and recognized in different degrees as invalids, because not one of the survivors was really in a very healthy state of body and spirit afterwards.

Some didn't have very far to go, used up. For those that were better and younger easy jobs were provided, portering like the Commissionaires and as cleaners on the "Wagon Lits" for the state transport catering services run by a privateer called "Peeters" who had the tender forever. I worked this out with the usual perseverance by keeping to the S.A.S. motto of "Who Dares Wins" most of the time.

Daniel and George just gave up: it was all over for them, it had been too much. No matter what I did to persuade them, because in my opinion they had all the rights that I had and could be paid back just the same way and combined as in war time. With our fresh experiences we could make a good bit of independent ventures still possible. An army truck would be given to us by the O.N.A.C. at a very reasonable rate, which we could convert to a refrigerated fish truck, transporting fish to inland sites. We could even get a three man trawler, the speediest in the harbor which later was ideal because of using two booms for trawling when permitted.

They let it all go for the fanfare with the girls to whoop it all up on their meagre sub existence level.

Barbaix was involved with the labor exchange since his demobilization and never got out of it except for his general hobbies in electricity and who knows what. I don't know how far that carried him but it looks like he led for the rest of his easy career a life of leisure. He got married and settled, finding it too much trouble to get his car out of the garage to meet a friend from long ago.

Daniel started his career from jail contacts after he was imprisoned for having emptied a couple of Army and Navy stores as an inside job, helped by and used by the British storekeeper. The Belgian Special Police or Gendarmes in cooperation with the British Military Police, giving himself away by his illustrious living splashed around in Cafes of ill repute with Madame and the girls giving away after pinching most of his loot from him when in a state of drunken debauchery.

17- An Aborted Act of Revenge:

Previously we had tried an abortive attempt to kidnap Leon Degrelle, a known Rexist, Blackshirt leader from his hospital in Bilbao, Spain, where he was temporarily in hiding having belly landed in a Dornier from the Eastern Front with other Nazis.

A face lift was going to be tried there for further transportation to South America, so we had to hurry up. The idea was to travel there with a fishing boat or small yacht to be purchased in Sable D'Olonne, where I had a friend named Coublanc, from Buchenwald.

We intended to land casually in Bilbao harbor after having visited Daniels Uncle in Pithivier and finding everybody had survived the last days too with hiding in the forest behind them, we continued towards the coast, the old route. Coublanc was back fishing working as a motorist on a trawler so he told us to stay with his wife and children. Daniel did that very well.

After visiting a few families around which weren't so lucky as us and a lot of tear shedding for their loved ones, who hadn't returned and which we might have been the last ones to have seen them, we returned to find there weren't enough funds left to acquire such a boat and having no sponsors for such a project in view we went back home where Daniel acted like Clark Gable before he turned himself in, after a chase jumping from the quay into a fishing boat, one of the cross ropes got him in the crotch and thus he appeared in the old dance hall.

The idea to bring Leon Dogrelle back for trial would also have been an act of justice, but at the same time may have vindicated him, taken in consideration with his war record which could have been revised Alas Daniel was not interested enough to be fully aware of it. I am sure an attempt could have been made with success had he been more serious.

Only a woman interested in his loose capers would later hold him to it, to walk straight. I think a social service for veterans could have done a lot of good too for lost souls like that.

18- On Making a Normal Life:

For myself Madame Denile had offered to help me to get a job on the Sabena as a radio operator or sparks after following the one year higher level institute in Brussels or Pursor on the mail boats, my Aunt Helen also trying to offer half share of my Uncle's plumbing business in the same area of Ixelles which was quite lucrative, after his untimely death.

I had a few other offers not quite so straightforward from my Aunt Ray and Cousin Irene who was married now to Bonnard as had been prearranged, to machine in his workshops in Morocco, Casablanca or Rabat or instead for a furniture removal firm with the run between Brussels and Paris.

I suppose I wanted to do my own bit which turned out to be the Merchant Navy for me instead.

My first ship was from Ghent, the S.S. Gella. They needed people that had completed the trade schools and motor engineering on trawlers for motormen as they were short of any kind of skilled tradesmen in those categories after the war.

My friend Roger and I studied the trawler exams. Roger had been taken over to England during the war and came back as a petty Officer from the Navy. In no time at all we were accepted and I started my short career in the Merchant Navy.

This ship was a beauty for its older make and twin motor capacity of 12,000 H.P. on each side. Called so after the ancient Viking call "Helle-a" before making and claiming a land. It was the speediest in the small fishing fleet because during the war it had been supplied with a Skoda motor which was too powerful so the insurance company wouldn't consider that until they changed the laws later on to fish with two trawler nets on each side.

She was manned in the same tradition then as now by Swedes, Norwegians, Danes, Dutch and Flemings to be tried and sold to the Chemical Union in Belgium with a destination of Morocco for phosphate and later to India to collect bones as there were many available there, then.

The try out was to find out how well the ship stood up to all conditions and of course the price. The greater the faults the lower the sales price. We carried some individuals on board who seemed pretty suspicious in their intentions.

The first voyage was characterized by one of the biggest storms in memory, in which we nearly were thrown back on the Isle of Wight, one side had conked out resulting in considerable loss of power; while turning in the wind and strong tides there to tackle up in it we nearly capsized, the boat being flimsily loaded with cement bags for ballast. The first engineer was a former Polish submarine Captain they said.

Anyway during the second wave, pondering, before we had time to right ourselves that was the crucial moment, I could see the dangerous angle in the engine room and a loose spare piston managed to jump out of its attachment missing us by a mere couple of feet.

The Polish engineer kept his hand up to give us a chance from the upper railings to make it for deck if necessary, when the ship started going back and not further down the danger level.

That had been a close one they told us later. Some of the inland mates aboard were nearer to tears than us, who started singing old but still known sea shanties, releasing our pent up feelings.
We liked it and felt proud of our sea spirits which we kept high, it was in the blood they used to say and with the salt spray in our hair and on our face, we sailed straight ahead at a steady pace towards Cherbourg for repairs in calmer waters near the harbor but still out at sea.

I could see Cherbourg from a different viewpoint than during the war the place of memories for me and events contributing to the landings later on.

John and the first engineer went with a pilot boat ashore and got some spare parts.

The damage was fixed up in no time and we could proceed towards the Gulf of Biscay having missed one of the worst hurricanes since 1927. I dried my washing in the middle of the Gulf thinking of one of my Uncles that had lost his life in different circumstances in the 1914 - 1918 war here. Their transport for troops had been torpedoed on its way to South West Africa in this approximate area. My uncle had knocked his head when one of the life boat ropes snapped and lost consciousness before hitting the water, somebody helped him for a while to keep afloat but to no avail.

I was a child when I heard the story in the old Cafe on the Sas and my Grandmother cried, she said young Edward could never swim the only one in the family and maybe it could have saved him.

Young Edward was a very good singer and the darling of the girls at the time. My Grandmother gave me his banjo, I never made good use of it, somehow it was all Edwards and I never could make a note on it but I loved it when my Dad did. From Cape Finisterre to Cape Hatteras on the Spanish coast of Galicia the Celtic part we sailed along noticing the fishing fleet had all their flags at half-mast. So many little boats were suddenly overwhelmed by this storm that had had no time to save themselves.

We entered Oporto to dock at Leixius where we noticed that a general strike was on, it was still the time of the Dictator. As we were the next day talking to a secret police aboard, suddenly the army appeared in vans and took the strikers away in them.

We asked the secret police what would happen to them, he answered they go on the next boat to Mozambique. Old ways die hard, here they were still very much alive.

Even Hano the Carthaginian is supposed to have recognized those parts before the destruction of Carthage by the Romans sailing as far as the Runeni River near South Africa, keeping the routes secret until some survivors from the cataclyst used it to escape under an Admiral called Habbakuk to vanish from the old world view completely and be forgotten for the time being.

With those thoughts I fell happily into a satisfied sleep with the certainty that the next morning I would find the first opportunity to jump ashore and explore the surrounding area, which I did with my mates.

Phosphate was blown into the holds and we would depart from Safi quicker than we envisaged.

We quickly explored the hills of the Atlas ending at the location we were at with the Sahara desert behind it.

We had to at least get a glimpse of one Camel with a hump to prove on a photo how many humps it had. A packet of camel cigarettes hadn't been very convincing, so the bet was on.

We actually found two camels with their drivers ready to enter the interior over the hills to join a caravan. The fellows posed for us and we placed the biggest disbeliever in the middle in front of the camel, so when the picture was developed the Dane blended in with the hump and we still couldn't see it.

After returning back to the ship and letting my cousin Irene in Casablanca know I was in Safi I met a Morocco veiled girl in the chemist shop guarded by two armed guards and one chaperone. Whilst the guards were outside and I tried on some sunglasses in the mirror she dropped her veil and the beauty of this girl was enchanting and also forbidden. Two other members of the crew had an unpleasant encounter at a mosque when they tried to enter, we later heard.

We rushed back to the ship not giving it anymore thought and took a last photo of a Moslem cemetery, amongst the roundish gravestones some were just headstones. I got stung by one of the cactus plants along the borders and this was painful, just like a bee sting. The ship was waiting and we sprang aboard ready to sail.
Later Irene had undertaken the 200 km. trip to meet me but gone like the wind the "Gella" took us back north, and as we knew it would return, the next trip would be to Casablanca anyway, I wrote her the news, back.

We arrived safely in Ghent at a bit of a tipping angle as the load had moved to one side on the high seas.

We had a bit of a mutiny going on as the daily meal was mutton and nothing but mutton every day, so we circled around from the kitchen in Indian file to the Captain bleating until we got the promise of a change in our diet. We went out in Ghent had a very good time and then went home.

Before the return trip we tried the lifeboats out and that was a bit of a trial, some were leaking, others were lacking plugs and pumps were not working.

In the Gulf of Biscay we floated around without power, until John had to swim down and under in the engine room to open the valves to release the water again that had come in, until everything worked again.

This time we went first to Lisbon and had a better time visiting the town with fair- grounds and Alexander bar. Our biggest difficulty was asking the way anywhere from Portuguese women who were very inhibited but we got there eventually and had a good time. Lisbon looked pretty new to us with the lift tram going up the sides.
Alongside the big seafarers statue we boarded the old "Cella" and sailed for the North African coast to make for Casablanca early in the morning this time.

There seemed to be a curfew and some trouble. I had no time to wait for the Purser and get an advance on my salary so I borrowed from my dear friends what I could gather in loose change and had a couple of cartons of American cigarettes tucked under the collar of a raincoat I had put over my arm, that was still the best collateral at that time. It worked plus my Belgian Passport.

Morocco was a protectorate of France becoming completely independent now from the issuing troubles and curfews: anyway I made for Irene's address not before getting some flowers, which to my surprise would have taken all my change when I asked the price, so I threw the bunch back to the Arab vendors and made a run for it taking no notice of the screaming sellers.

Arriving at the house they told me that Irene was at the cinema so I bought my way in with a packet of cigarettes and found her with the aid of the usher.

Her welcome was warm and hospitable after all this time. I told her I was engaged and she responded that my first daughter should be called Irene, my second daughter eventually was so called.

I cannot remember the names of her children. The last thing we did was visiting some other family from my Grandfather's side namely a son of his sister Valery, who was running a sales and supply store for the factories in Lille and Roubaix belonging to the husband of his sister, Baron Van Monchoven, whom she had married in 1918 who was an officer in the French Army. His castle and country manor was in Peque, which was still on Belgian soil, the demarcation line having split his properties and loyalties from one to the other.

196

What reminiscences, hearing of the old Aunts and Uncles again with those typically old names. Anyway we thought the reception was rather cool and reserved considering and I wonder today whether I have got any family at all.

Even Irene for reasons unknown to me managed to get estranged from me. The only thing I remember when I left Casablanca was I had a last look at the Casbah where during the French protection the French lived in the European part and the Moroccans mostly over the rail tracks. Previously Irene told me there was even a wooden wall separating the two sections.

In the Casbah lots of men were walking hand in hand, which was usual Irene said, she also warned me to watch out for venereal disease if I should go with any Arab girls as most of them had it, without the real after effects we would get.

Well that was a good bit of advice and later we heard that the Atlantic plateau between Safi and Agadir had moved upwards and caused an earthquake that killed at least two thousand people. A good thing we were away from there at that moment. With those terrible tidings I left Morocco and never heard any more of my family. Some are in Belgium, France and England but no contact, what a pity. It's like a whole generation has died out and gone into oblivion. They all had to plot together in three's again as I was foretold, making big gravestones for each other from the various monies and just disappeared.

What I lost in the process wasn't worth talking about in real terms just the injustice of it, but it would have come in handy to bring up a big family on my own. We made it struggling wherever I came and went still managing to give my band the essentials of life for which I am very grateful.

On the return to Ghent Roger and I made it back to Ostend to be taken on the Congo boats for the Maritime Belge in Antwerp. This sent us off to Angola and the Congo, I went to Lobito and Roger to Matadi in the Congo stream. A climate Roger couldn't tolerate and he became allergic too, becoming covered in big boils all over. That was his career finished, he got married and forever stayed ashore.
For me it was only the starting I thought, the sea was good to me, good money, a home and an appetite like a horse.

Coming up to fourth engineer I would have to go to the Engineers School again, in Antwerp unless I choose to stay aspirant or motorist. For the time being prospects looked good. So we sailed to begin with on the same route, slightly knocked a ship on the bow coming across us towards Zebrugge like a slowpoke. The same turning around like a drifting and rudderless hopeless victim demanded a parley with our captain.

As the damage wasn't too bad they decided it was O.K. and off we went past old Morocco now to the Deep South with past memories coming to the fore.

Our ship was pretty new and called "Galopin" after a Governor, and was speedy, equipped for the tropics and could take cargo and one hundred passengers. It was equipped with an enormous five cylinder engine, producing tremendous H.P. and it also had coolers for tropical fruits.

We carried factory installations and in return copper ore from the Katanga over the Benguela rail track to Lobito. We took Paladrine against the scourge of Malaria and drank the best of Simba beer brewed in the Congo, food was excellent we all had ships officer's uniforms when on leave.

After Tenerife for two hours bunkering we left the channel between Dakar and the Cape Verde Islands, that's when you didn't sleep on deck because of health reasons, that's when the flies came on board, it once was the graveyard of sailors. Now most of the swamps ashore are filled in. We kept under the protection of our fans in the cabins and our pills that made us for three days so tired that we could hardly lift a hammer. Sweating and drinking with the continuous blowing of the ventilation on us.
The Gulf of Guinea was soon reached and crossed, watching the flying fish like herrings with wings flying aboard and alongside the ship we had sharks. In this manner Lobito soon appeared in our sight and that was the first view of real Africa, heat crude hills, a boy blaring away , huts on the far slopes, a fort with the Portuguese flag flapping in the hot breeze. Ranchers with big felt hats, leopard skins and cattle skins on the quay tied in big bundles and smelling very much.
African fires everywhere emitting an aroma of smoky tropical wood, colorful poinsettias everywhere and cicada's chirping away in the trees.

Nice Mulatto girls, wares on their heads passing by, a lovely lagoon with sandy beach and a row of bungalows cutting off harbor from sea. At night the whole scene came alive. Noise of the Toms-Toms "Sabuchie" as they called it, dancing whirling, singing and drinking, from the big township in the hills nearby in between the banana plantations, where the bananas grew as big as one's arm. We eagerly picked them up from the market next day.

We hired an Austin car the next day paying for it between us and went inland looking at the hunters coming back with their newly acquired trophies of Zebras, Leopards and Lions on their cars.

We watched a river where its toll of human lives was taken regularly from children fetching water or swimming by the crocodiles.

We wasted two hours of our precious time waiting for an old African Tribesman with spear and all nonchalantly holding us up on a single rail track bridge for a train coming from out of nowhere, before we hit those wild hills, and then it was time to return, same procedure as before.

In the evening we relaxed on, one of the outside terraces absorbing all the African noises in with a cool drink, listening to an Afrikaner from Carolina and his tales of the Transvaal.
We weren't allowed into the cinema because we had no jackets on, the Portuguese kept up their rules and all the mulatto beauties for themselves.

A Norwegian cargo ship managed to suddenly blaze up in the harbor, showing us the silhouettes of the shark fins sailing by under our very noses and big fish suddenly jumping out near the beach at the other side. Thousands scurrying away in the dark on the beach.

Before sailing away we bought stocks of cane sugar, big bags of it, and crocodile skins and hid it all between engine and in gullies to sell some in the Canaries, and took colorful shawls and silver works from there to Belgium; all fruits were in great demand, and we took some with us in the secret holds to ripen nicely on our way to the cool temperate zones where they were unloaded on the side the next day, in small boats in the dock, to alleviate the shortages the country was still suffering from after the devastating war we had all gone through.

Anyway I felt that I was truly well back into useful service fighting my own way back without having to go to rest places to recuperate in the Limburg and Switzerland.

I also fought my own free way back into life's competition with the best and held my head high without flinging to the weak side and bribes, I even passed an exam for the stores and magazines of the mail boats with flying colors, but they waited too long to let me know.

I undertook a last trip with the Govenor Galopin and we pulled a burned out piston of the mains motor without the help of a shore maintenance crew or crane equipment available in Lobito. It had to be achieved by a hundred boys pulling in line singing their tribal songs helping us splendidly, which was a bit of a record for the first engineer, telling to us on the trip back how a propeller was changed in mid sea which was recorded in the annals of the company in Antwerp, we listened amazed as I brought the bananas in from the freezer which we had intended to eat before he had interrupted us saying he didn't like them.

He had a bad history by now of ulcers like all first engineers with all their worries and the fumes.

My stomach had its repercussions too, thin lining from starvation which never really bettered and typhoid fever I found out at a later date. So we were all in the same boat anyway.

One day I was called at midday only for one hour to replace a young recruit from Ostend who said he didn't feel well, it turned out to be a frame-up as one of the cylinders and rings were melted on to the auxiliary motor because they hadn't had the service of the recruit during his shift.

No matter what I said it didn't put it right and was a perfect setup between Ferrier, the recruit, and the first engineer I soon found out, because we had three more auxiliary motors to use for convenience and starting the big motor, electricity etc. while we repairing this seeing he had just repaired the big one with all the credit attributable.

It was no odds for me at all and my fiancée Yvonne, my soul mate, asked me to come and get married in London. Previous to that I on one of my voyages home had made a quick dash to England just for one night to become engaged to Yvonne having purchased an engagement ring in Antwerp with my first months' salary from the ship.

The hall was booked the guests invited and the cake brought from South Africa, things in Europe still being hard to get. We had a special license, Belgium seeming slow with permission due to their Napoleonic Laws, I was 25 years old and the notice had been put in the Town Hall of Ostend. Foreigners need authorization when out of their own land at that time, and it had to be when Yvonne's father was home from his ship which was just for 2 weeks. In the end we went to Church House Westminster and I swore on the bible and became an accepted Anglican and was married in John Keble Church Mill Hill with friends and family around.

My career in the Navy was over and I could look forward to a shore life with all the responsibilities of a large family which ended up with four lovely girls and one boy.

Abroad and competing doubly, I managed to concentrate my acquired engineering skills for working in garages and machine shops in factories which were in full swing at that time with bonuses and lots of overtime.

I even received a nine month rehabilitation course in Ghent for garage management in the higher technical institutes for veterans and alike, under which I qualified, which entitled me to luxuries by now as I was paid out like a professional in damage claims. I received a political cross from Prince Albert with four stars and had the right of the Order of Leopold.

My absence eventually got me out of touch with all the news as the last appeal closed in 1953 when I embarked on trying to improve myself with work and making a home for my family.

I was called back about a year after the exams to start in the workshops of the mail boats which I couldn't do as I had left for Canada and with my travels I wasn't even able to attend my Mother's or Uncle's funerals, I did make it for my Dads as I was living in England again at that time. An unfair distribution of my inheritance had already taken place before my arrival.

So I lost all trace of my family and benefits, I was either in England, Canada or Rhodesia at the time.

Working hard still bringing the family up nothing was ever short, prospecting and mining for which I took further studies, and being involved in between the war of Settlers and Freedom Fighters, minding my own business as much as I could to get on independently and holding on to the right for freedom of expression, I had so much endeavored and hungered for during the war period which was always fresh in my memory.

I find that the African situation cannot entirely be put in the same situation as our struggle against the enemy occupation either.

Old and new Settlers have had a hard survival struggle in making something of their own out of those primitive conditions we all once upon a time faced whether that was in the New World or in other even more primitive places elsewhere. I should say that is similar in many ways. They brought wealth to those places in skills and ambitions with employment and often with their own finances as well.

There was potential there, but before everything it had to be implemented and achieved.

The situations were hard and tough, difficult to overcome. The offspring that was begat fully earned their laurels, the native populations improved mostly with their emergence from their own dark age that previously they had been under.

The so called emancipation brought to life from big blokes having received theirs under completely different circumstances and hardships does not apply at all, and they are far less concerned about the advancement of their so called protégés, as they call it, than the local settlers that have done more than the so called meddling do-good who only brought hardship and troubles in return on a massive scale, while those very same people have no good example in their own countries of having solved their own still present troubles of a similar nature far worse in relation to numbers and potential.

Those are the true findings of people who bear the scars of unjust wars, who survived in the loins of generations of their ancestors who reached that conclusion. Only wisdom and the necessary will enable us to understand and turn this world into a paradise for all.

"Jedem das Seine", "To Each His Own" will once more remind us of this.

202

Made in the USA
Las Vegas, NV
07 May 2021